"If you've ever wondere[d] please pick up this book! [...] reminds women that we don't have to be 'enough,' because Christ is enough for us and in us. Dive into these chapters to find encouragement and peace as Denisse points to the truths of the gospel."

Lauren McAfee, author of *Only One Life* and *Not What You Think*; ministry coordinator at Hobby Lobby Corporate

"*Set Apart* is an extraordinary message that leads us to rediscover our unique calling and identity in Christ. No matter where you are or where you've been, Denisse Copeland's powerful words rooted in the truth of Scripture will help you find greater courage, clearer vision, and stronger faith. We live in confusing times, but God's calling for you to be set apart is clearer than ever. Read this book! You'll be so glad you did."

Dave and Ashley Willis, authors of *The Naked Marriage* and hosts of *The Naked Marriage Podcast*

"Reading this book was like sitting with a girlfriend over a cup of coffee and leaving feeling refreshed and strengthened. The comparison game is exhausting and does not lead us to peace and joy. If you're tired of striving, worrying, and comparing, read this book and share it with someone you love."

Ines S. Franklin, teaching pastor at Mariners Church, Irvine, CA; founder of Trochia Ministries

"Denisse's heart is so evident that reading her story will leave you feeling refreshed, recharged, and renewed. Her words are like sweet, warm honey over a hurting heart. If you're ready for real life change and to finally walk in who God says you are, you need to read this book."

Tiffany Rogers, blogger and life coach

"No matter where you are starting from, God wants to help you live the most incredible set-apart life. Denisse is amazing, and she has so many important stories to share that will deeply affect your faith. She will help you see that God has a great plan and purpose for you—one that will set you apart and be so amazing—starting right where you are in your everyday life."

Matt Brown, evangelist, author of *Truth Plus Love*, and founder of Think Eternity

"Have you ever longed for a big sister, mentor, or honest friend to encourage and guide you through the ongoing struggles of life? Look no further. Through relatable and engaging stories and with solid biblical principles, Denisse will draw you in gently, leaving you with a greater hunger for the transforming power of God's Word and the overwhelming love of Jesus."

Alisha Illian, author of *Chasing Perfect* and founder of Women RePurposed

SET APART

SET APART

Stop Comparing, Own Your Giftedness, and Rest in Jesus

DENISSE COPELAND

BakerBooks

a division of Baker Publishing Group
Grand Rapids, Michigan

© 2021 by Denisse Copeland

Published by Baker Books
a division of Baker Publishing Group
PO Box 6287, Grand Rapids, MI 49516-6287
www.bakerbooks.com

Printed in the United States of America

Library of Congress Cataloging-in-Publication Data
Names: Copeland, Denisse, 1995– author.
Title: Set apart : stop comparing, own your giftedness, and rest in Jesus / Denisse Copeland.
Description: Grand Rapids, Michigan : Baker Books, a division of Baker Publishing Group, [2021] | Includes bibliographical references.
Identifiers: LCCN 2020058684 | ISBN 9781540901026 (paperback) | ISBN 9781540901712 (casebound) | ISBN 9781493430260 (ebook)
Subjects: LCSH: Christian women—Religious life.
Classification: LCC BV4527 .C664 2021 | DDC 248.8/43—dc23
LC record available at https://lccn.loc.gov/2020058684

Unless otherwise indicated, Scripture quotations are from THE HOLY BIBLE, NEW INTERNATIONAL VERSION®. NIV®. Copyright © 1973, 1978, 1984, 2011 by Biblica, Inc.™ Used by permission. All rights reserved worldwide.

Scripture quotations labeled BSB are from The Berean Bible (www.Berean.Bible), Berean Study Bible (BSB) © 2016–2020 by Bible Hub and Berean.Bible. Used by permission. All rights reserved.

Scripture quotations labeled ESV are from The Holy Bible, English Standard Version® (ESV®), copyright © 2001 by Crossway, a publishing ministry of Good News Publishers. Used by permission. All rights reserved. ESV Text Edition: 2016

Scripture quotations labeled ISV are from the International Standard Version, Copyright © 1995–2014 by ISV Foundation. All rights reserved internationally. Used by permission of Davidson Press, LLC.

Scripture quotations labeled MSG are from THE MESSAGE, copyright © 1993, 2002, 2018 by Eugene H. Peterson. Used by permission of NavPress. All rights reserved. Represented by Tyndale House Publishers, Inc.

Scripture quotations labeled NCV are from the New Century Version®. Copyright © 2005 by Thomas Nelson. Used by permission. All rights reserved.

Scripture quotations labeled NKJV are from the New King James Version®. Copyright © 1982 by Thomas Nelson. Used by permission. All rights reserved.

Scripture quotations labeled NLT are from the *Holy Bible*, New Living Translation, copyright © 1996, 2004, 2007, 2013, 2015 by Tyndale House Foundation. Used by permission of Tyndale House Publishers, Inc., Carol Stream, Illinois 60188. All rights reserved.

Italics added to Scripture quotations reflect the author's emphasis.

The author is represented by MacGregor & Luedeke Literary.

21 22 23 24 25 26 27   7 6 5 4 3 2 1

I dedicate this book to Jesus Christ,
the Son of God,
for teaching and showing us how to live
as a set-apart people for his glory.

CONTENTS

INTRODUCTION

Our Set-Apart Sisterhood

"RASHAWN, can you help me straighten the house?" I called.

"I'm watching a sermon, babe, but I'll help you when I'm done," my husband answered.

I looked at the clock. Less than an hour till Bible study started. The clock was ticking, and I was ticking with it! I was pregnant, tired, and getting madder by the second.

We host a Bible study at our house on Thursday nights. Every week I prepare by trying to create an environment of peace and love. I want people to enter our home and feel at rest. Whenever someone walks in, I want them to feel welcomed. It's tough to lovingly welcome people when my mind's spinning on all the cooking, cleaning, laundry, and parenting stuff I didn't get done, so I try to finish all that ahead of time. That way I can focus solely on hosting others once Bible study starts.

This Thursday had been an extra busy one. Rashawn was at work all day, so it was just me and our son Aiden in the house. Me, a toddler, and a pile of things to do. Not a great combo. My goal was to get everything done before Bible study, but then . . .

You know how it goes. Our baby was extra cranky. Unexpected issues came up. Dinnertime rolled around, and Rashawn came home. We had less than an hour till the guests showed up, and the house was a disaster. Like, an *actual* disaster.

That's when I asked Rashawn for help.

And he answered that he was watching a sermon! How do I argue with that? *He's listening to the Word of God,* I reasoned. But I also fumed inwardly: *All I'm asking for is help straightening up the house; I don't think I'm crazy!*

Clearly, I wasn't going to get any help from him, so I went into turbo mode, knocking it out myself, though with less of a cheerful spirit than I care to remember. Angry thoughts boiled in my mind: *I'm so tired. This is too much, but no one else is going to get it done, so I guess it's up to me . . . again.*

All the while, there was my husband, listening to a sermon to prep for Bible study. I love that Rashawn is a man of God's Word, but didn't he see how much I needed his help? By the time people arrived, I felt drained. Even though hosting is one of my primary spiritual gifts, that night I had worked myself into a fury of anxiety and frustration.

Been There, Done That

Have you ever been there? Working, working, *working*—maybe toward a really good purpose—and ending up drained, frustrated, and exhausted? You're not alone. The Gospel of Luke records the story of a woman in the same situation:

As Jesus and his disciples were on their way, he came to a village where a woman named Martha opened her home to him. She had a sister called Mary, who sat at the Lord's feet listening to what he said. But Martha was distracted by all the preparations that had to be made. She came to him and asked, "Lord, don't you care that my sister has left me to do the work by myself? Tell her to help me!"

"Martha, Martha," the Lord answered, "you are worried and upset about many things, but few things are needed—or indeed only one. Mary has chosen what is better, and it will not be taken away from her." (Luke 10:38–42)

According to this passage of Scripture, that night—while I was freaking out about the house and Rashawn was sitting in his office listening to a sermon—my husband had chosen what was better! Just like Mary, Rashawn chose to sit at Jesus's feet and learn instead of getting distracted by an ever-expanding to-do list.

Reading this, you might respond with exasperation. *What am I supposed to do—not care when company comes over? Does choosing "what's better" mean reading my Bible and praying all day? Who's supposed to cook? Who's gonna clean? How will anything get done?*

Sister, I understand! I can completely relate. And I'm not saying I was wrong to want to create an environment of peace and warmth in our home that Thursday night. God has gifted me as a hostess, and I know he wants me to use that gifting for his glory and to bless others. He also wants me to use my talents for him without strain and striving, anger and anxiety. In Luke 10, Jesus was addressing the heart behind Mary's and Martha's actions.

I wonder how much anxiety we could avoid in life if we learned to live as Mary did. To let go of unhealthy expectations and the fear of disappointing people. To rest in confidence that we are enough instead of getting caught in the pile of tasks to complete.

Doesn't freedom, rest, and confidence in Christ sound good?

In this book, I want us to learn together. I want us to choose what's better, to live so close to Jesus that using our gifts for his glory is a joy, not just one more thing we have to do.

While we learn together about sitting at Jesus's feet, I also want us to consider another aspect of the story recorded in Luke 10. While Jesus does say that Mary chose what was better that night, I think we often forget that we can learn from Martha too.

Both sisters had unique giftings, and both their lives hold lessons for us. Jesus set apart both Mary and Martha for his kingdom work, and in Christ we are part of the same set-apart sisterhood.

Our ancient sister Martha worked to serve her guests. That's a good thing! She had the gift of hospitality, and she was living it out. But when she strayed into overworking herself for the benefit of others, she lost sight of her own spiritual needs. Mary, on the other hand, was focused on receiving encouragement from Jesus and gaining spiritual nourishment as she listened to him. She was exactly where she needed to be at that time. However, those around her could have easily looked down on her for her lack of hospitality or support for her sister. When we vilify one woman and put the other on a pedestal, we miss out on learning lessons God can teach us through *both* of them.

Each sister had strengths and weaknesses. Each has much to teach us.

I don't know about you, but I can relate to Mary *and* Martha. There are times—like that fateful Thursday night Bible study—when I feel like Martha, so anxious to finish everything, so anxious to have things just right for our guests. But there are also times when I'm like Mary, sitting at Jesus's feet and learning from him. Both are needed. But how do we find balance between serving God with our whole heart and sitting at Jesus's feet?

There is a way, and through this book I'm inviting you to join me on the journey.

The Way of Enough

As women, we face so many questions. *Am I doing enough? Am I good enough? Will I ever feel like I'm enough?*

Answering these questions was complicated enough when I was single. Then I got married, and a whole new set of concerns flooded my mind. *Am I helping Rashawn enough with his job? Have I asked lately if he needs help? Are we doing enough ministry?*

As if this complexity wasn't enough, then I became a parent. I thought my brain would explode with questions: *Does Aiden have the right number of wet diapers? Why is he crying? Has he been burped enough? Is he comfortable?* And with the birth of our second son, Eliyah, the questions just kept coming: *Am I giving my kids enough healthy food? Am I teaching them enough about Jesus? Am I loving them like I should? Am I getting enough quality time with Aiden now that Eliyah's here? How am I ever going to be enough for them?*

All the while, questions about my own heart lurked in the quiet corners of my mind: *Am I praying enough? Am I worshiping enough? Am I pleasing God? Do I need to reach out to a sister in Christ to see how she is? Should I be reaching out to another mom to see if she needs help? Am I closing myself off because I've been so busy and overwhelmed?*

So many things to worry about! So much to take care of! Beneath all of these questions lies the root question: *Am I enough?*

I don't know about you, but I've had enough of enough!

There has to be a better way, a way beyond the deep fear that if we don't do it right, everything will fall apart or we'll miss out. That life could be better if we just worked harder. People would love us more. Our kids would be happier. Friends would drop by more often. Our marriage would be better. Just keep working, working, working.

But what if it's the opposite? What if the things we're chasing, the things we're hoping will settle all the "good enough" questions, are actually the *source* of our exhaustion?

Remember, in the story of Mary and Martha, Jesus doesn't chide Martha for being a hostess. He doesn't say, "Don't clean your house. Don't cook for guests." He simply says Mary has chosen what is *better.*

What if, by trying to hold it all together, we're missing out? Jesus says, "Come to me, all you who are weary and burdened, and I will give you rest" (Matt. 11:28). Rest. Peace. Isn't that what we all need?

That Thursday night before Bible study, my chores felt like a giant weight on me. I wanted to get things done my way, in my strength. I was pursuing what I thought was best—a clean house, comfortable guests, and happy children. But I was missing out on what was truly best. Martha was doing good things too, but she was doing them from mixed motives. She may have wanted to please Jesus, but she also had a worldly view of what was *enough* that evening. She didn't see that it was enough to be at Jesus's feet.

Like Martha, you and I can't effectively operate in our gifting if we're serving with an anxious heart. We can't be our best if we're stressing over the details. We can't give God all the glory when we're trying to please everyone around us.

So I'll ask you: Why do you do the things you do? What drives you?

Is it comparing yourself to others? Fear? A search for purpose, for meaning, for a sense of *enough?*

Do you know what God has gifted you to do? Do you know how to use those gifts for his glory, without worry, approval seeking, and exhaustion?

We've been set apart to know Christ, to sit at his feet. We've also been set apart to serve him with everything we are—heart, soul, mind, and strength. We can never enjoy our identity as beloved, set-apart daughters if we don't learn that, in Jesus, we are already enough.

Throughout the pages of this book, I hope you'll discover this truth with me. Knowing and actually *living out* the truth that in Christ we are already and always enough helps us use everything we have—our resources, our giftings, our very lives—to bring God the glory that he's due.

In the first few chapters, we'll look at how life changes when we work from a new identity, from worship, and from prayer. Then we'll look at some dangers to avoid—comparison, approval-seeking, and anxiety. Finally, we'll explore what it means to live like we're enough—being known by, loved by, and truly satisfied in Jesus.

He has something much better for us than checking off an endless to-do list or worrying about whether we should push more and try harder. He offers us himself. He is the Prince of Peace, the God who does not drive us but draws us. In him we find rest and the confidence that we are enough.

You, dear sister, are enough.

Anytime you read that phrase—*you are enough*—in this book, I want you to rejoice in, rest in, and understand the truth. When I say you are enough, I'm not trying to inflate your self-esteem or puff you up. Self-help and motivational pep talks from me would only harm you in the end.

Instead, when I affirm *you are enough*, I am pointing you to the eternal truth that, because of Jesus's sacrifice for your sins and based on your confession of him as Lord of your life, you lack nothing. You have nothing to prove. You are unconditionally loved and accepted. Scripture tells us that we can do nothing apart from Christ, but that in him we can do all things (John 15:5; Phil. 4:13).

In Jesus, *you are enough.*

If, like me, you ever have trouble believing that, then let's journey together. Together in Christ, I know we'll discover strength to tackle life head-on. We'll start living fully out of who God has made us to be. If you're ready for that, let's dive in.

1

SET APART
IS WHO WE ARE

I GREW UP IN PUERTO RICO, where I was raised on beans and rice, plantains, hospitality, and hard work. I love my country—the island breezes, the sound of the waves lapping or crashing on the shore, the colors and flavors and culture. The beauty of my home can hardly be expressed in words.

My family life, however, can be summed up in one word: broken.

My parents divorced when I was very young. Seeking a better life, my dad moved to Florida, leaving my sister and me behind. As a child, I often felt confused, alone, even unwanted.

I didn't understand why I couldn't have a normal family. Of course, I didn't know exactly what "normal" meant, but I longed for stability and security. I didn't want to wonder if the boyfriend I was introduced to one day would be my stepdad the next. I didn't want to argue all the time. I didn't want to deal with the nagging feeling that everyone liked my sister better than me.

Though my home country has a strongly religious culture, and most Puerto Ricans would say they believe in God, I didn't see many people connected to Christ in a real or personal way. Without the grounding love of Jesus, I never learned to love myself. I needed someone to teach me.

Instead, I learned about anger. And alcohol. And pain. Though I hurt so often, I didn't know any different. I grew up thinking, "This is just how things are."

After Dad moved to Florida, it was hard for us to visit him. He remarried and had two children, which widened the gap between us. Even though I didn't get to see him very much growing up, I've always been a daddy's girl. Whenever I did visit, it was always great. We would occasionally spend vacations with him for extended quality time together. But his distance made my already broken life more painful.

Growing up, I never felt treasured or chosen. In many ways, I had an orphan heart.

Stumbling in the Dark

By the time I hit high school, I'd finally had enough. I packed my luggage and left. I'm not sure if I hoped someone would beg me to stay, but no one did. First my grandma took me in. Then my dad filed for custody. *Things will be better in America,* I convinced myself.

Once my dad gained custody of my sister and me, we went to live with him in Florida. I arrived in the United States in time for my junior and senior years of high school, but there was a big problem: I knew hardly any English. School was so, so hard.

Using my sloppy English, I figured things out in school and managed to graduate. To receive my diploma, however, I had to jump through a final hoop of passing a standardized test in English. Though I studied and practiced and took the test over and over again, I never passed. Without that diploma, my dream of going to college crashed and burned.

Since I wasn't eligible for college, I went straight to work. While working, I met a girl who became my best friend. I vented to her about how hard it was for me to understand my dad's ways. He strictly enforced a curfew and so many other rules; I just wanted to be free. Free to do whatever I wanted. Free to not have to tell anybody where I was. She invited me to live with her, so I packed up my stuff and moved in with her family. *Finally*, I thought, *I'll have all the freedom I want.*

This girl had a bit of a faith background, but she didn't live out of a love relationship with Jesus. Her father, though, was a truly committed Christian. In opening the door to their home, my friend's parents opened my heart to faith. But things got worse before they got better.

Once I moved in with this family, everything seemed to fall apart. My car started breaking down, which put a strain on my finances. And I was in a crazy relationship—such a disaster, really. My boyfriend verbally abused me, but I didn't know who I was as a woman, so I clung to the relationship. Over and over, I put my identity in all the wrong places, all the wrong relationships. I partied, smoked, and drank. I did whatever I wanted, and I wanted to explore and experience new things.

Looking back, I see how desperately I was searching for an identity, trying to see where I fit in the world. I dressed like the world, partied like the world, and posed like the world. Social media became a place where I could show off what I had. I spent time working out, tanning, and keeping up with the latest trends and culture. I did all I could to receive the attention and validation that I never received as a child. If you were to look at my life from the outside, you would have thought I had everything together. But inside I was searching . . . anxious . . . unsettled.

When the opportunity to do some modeling presented itself, I jumped at the chance. What girl doesn't want to feel beautiful enough to be a model? I wanted to be seen and known for what I had to offer. Trouble was, I kept having to give more—even if it meant my body. I modeled lingerie, posing seductively for the camera. I just so badly wanted to feel like I was *enough*, but I never did.

As my dating relationship got worse and worse, my best friend invited me to a Bible study. She wanted to get me out of this horrible situation and around positive people. So I went. Even though she wasn't serving Christ with her life, she knew I needed Jesus. And I did—so, so much.

The Bible study was at a coffee shop in Brooksville, Florida. I showed up at seven o'clock one night—no Bible, no notebook, nothing! I just sat there and took it all in. Something felt so different about the way these people talked and shared with one another. That first night, I couldn't understand what they were saying or the words they were reading. All I knew was that there was peace. I felt safe.

A couple nights after that first Bible study, I finally broke up with my boyfriend. I remember driving home from his house at three o'clock in the morning after the breakup. No other cars dotted the road, just me. Pulling up to a stoplight, I finally broke down crying. I started talking to God—at least I tried to. I didn't even know if he could hear me or not, but I just remember saying, "I'm sorry."

Though I didn't know what repentance was, I started telling God I was sorry for all the stuff that I'd done. I felt like all of the bad things in my life were happening to me because of what I'd done to other people. I thought it was all coming back to haunt me. Stuff I thought I had forgotten about came flooding back to me. I poured out my heart, crying and wrestling. Afterward, this overwhelming peace rested on me. Everything was washed clean, and I felt new. Humbled and grateful, I drove home to my best friend's house.

I kept going to Bible study, and the leaders switched from meeting in a coffee shop to meeting in someone's home. At that house church, I finally gave my life to Christ. We were going through Francis Chan's book and video series *Crazy Love*. Chan asked the question, "If God were on one knee proposing to you, and the ring was Jesus, would you marry him?" That question rocked me to my core. I said yes and gave my life to the Lord.

A New Identity

Everything started changing . . . and fast. Before Christ, my life spun in out-of-control circles; once I gave my life to the Lord, doors began to open. Slowly, as I spent time in his Word, the Lord started showing me my true identity in him. My heart awakened to truth. I became fully alive in the power of the Holy Spirit. I had moved from spiritual death to abundant life.

Before I accepted Jesus as my Savior, a brother in Christ from my house church gave me a Bible. He encouraged me to read Psalm 1, so I did.

> Blessed is the one
>> who does not walk in step with the wicked
> or stand in the way that sinners take
>> or sit in the company of mockers,
> but whose delight is in the law of the LORD,
>> and who meditates on his law day and night.
> That person is like a tree planted by streams of water,
>> which yields its fruit in season
> and whose leaf does not wither—
>> whatever they do prospers.
>
> Not so the wicked!
>> They are like chaff
>> that the wind blows away.
> Therefore the wicked will not stand in the judgment,
>> nor sinners in the assembly of the righteous.
>
> For the LORD watches over the way of the righteous,
>> but the way of the wicked leads to destruction.
>>> (Ps. 1:1–6)

"What do you think it means?" he asked.

I honestly had no idea. I could not understand the words. He started explaining the psalm, but even then I couldn't grasp the meaning. This wasn't a problem with my English. I simply couldn't comprehend who or what he was talking about; I wasn't yet alive in Christ.

After I accepted Jesus, I went back and read Psalm 1 again. Its meaning exploded in my mind. I understood that these words described *me*! I had been the wicked one. I was doing things outside of God's will, things that displeased and dishonored him. I was doing everything the psalm talked about: walking in step with the wicked, standing with sinners, sitting in the company of mockers. When Jesus died for sin, he died for this sin . . . *my* sin. Because his death and resurrection gave me new life, I could live like the righteous, planted by streams of water, bearing fruit and never withering.

The Holy Spirit showed me what his Word meant. That's how the Holy Spirit works; he brings us out of darkness and into light. Then he teaches us to discern the difference.

Life without Christ is like being in a very dark room. You can't see any of the furniture. You don't know where the walls are. You bump into everything, and it hurts, but you can't see where you are or what you're doing. Then someone turns on the light, and suddenly you can see what was there all along. For those who no longer desire spiritual darkness, the Holy Spirit turns on the light. As God fanned the flame of faith in me, I marveled at how much Jesus changed my life. I no longer felt so bumped, bruised, and heartbroken from stumbling in the dark.

My Set-Apart Identity

As I've told you, prior to surrendering my life to Jesus, I constantly wondered if I was enough. I searched for love and identity everywhere, but nothing satisfied me. That lack of love and purpose was the root of all my struggles.

Orphaned through the abandonment and abuse I felt as a child, caught in a web of toxic relationships with others, I thought the only answer was to give more, to try harder.

Every time I gave part of myself away—to a boyfriend, to the camera, at a party—I hoped I would finally find peace. I wanted love. I wanted purpose. But it wasn't until I tasted and saw that the Lord is good (Ps. 34:8) that my identity began to take shape.

Jesus showed me that I am enough in his sight. He did this by accepting and receiving me just as I was, broken and lost. He saw every part of me and loved me unconditionally. He required nothing of me but to yield to his love and mercy. I wanted to feel like enough to the world, but instead I discovered that in God's eyes I had always been enough. I had nothing left to prove.

Becoming a Christian and experiencing Jesus's love overwhelmed me with grace and peace. Now, as long as I have the Father's love, what happens can't shake me. That's not to say that I don't hurt when trials come my way; pain is still part of my life! It's just different with Jesus. I'm in him. I'm his beloved daughter. I'm set apart for his purposes. I'm not an orphan anymore, because Christ reconciled me to my precious heavenly Father.

Feeling like an orphan had led me nowhere. For so many years I had lived in fear, trying everything to earn people's love, or at least to keep them from being angry with me. Over and over, I thought, "If I do *this*, they'll love me." It seemed to me that there were endless conditions to love. But that's not the way God our heavenly Father parents or loves us. If you're a daughter or a son of the King of kings, you are free. You don't have to hide anything or pretend to be someone you're not. As a beloved, set-apart child of God, you can run to your Father and ask him for anything. His unconditional love will never fail you.

When he came to earth, Jesus lived like this before God his Father. Even in childhood, Jesus knew where his identity was found. One time, when he was twelve, Jesus traveled with his parents to Jerusalem for Passover. After the festival ended, their party left to return home to Nazareth, but Joseph and Mary realized Jesus wasn't with them. So they went back to Jerusalem to search for their son. When they finally found him in the temple and chided him for getting separated from them, Jesus answered, "Didn't you know I had to be in my Father's house?" (Luke 2:49). Even at the young age of twelve, Jesus had complete confidence in his identity as the Son of God.

At thirty years old, Jesus began his ministry by being baptized in the Jordan River. As he came up from the water, "the Holy Spirit descended on him in bodily form like a dove. And a voice came from heaven: 'You are my Son, whom I love; with you I am well pleased'" (Luke 3:22). Every step of Jesus's ministry was marked by his identity as a beloved Son. Imagine growing up with that kind of confidence! Jesus knew—without a shadow of a doubt—that he was enough in his Father's eyes.

The incredible truth is that we don't have to imagine it; we can live it!

When we become God's children, we receive the same kind of confidence Jesus had to approach God as our Father, knowing he loves us. Through his death and resurrection, Christ has forgiven all our sins. And Jesus is the *only* reason we're enough. I am enough because Jesus died for me. Nothing I ever did made me feel enough or valuable. But the precious blood of Christ, shed for me on Calvary, settles forever the question of whether I'm enough. His death and new life settles that question for you too.

I wonder if Mary felt this sweetness of being a beloved, set-apart daughter as she sat at Jesus's feet in Luke 10. I imagine joy filled her from just being with him. There's certainly a reason she insisted on being with Jesus instead of helping Martha with the chores. His presence was a rare treat, and she wanted to soak it up! She had finally found love that accepted her perfectly, brokenness and all. She had finally found wisdom that made sense of life, healing from tears and heartache, and hope through God's forgiveness.

Sitting and listening was the only way Mary could hear Jesus's words. Remember, the New Testament wasn't written yet, so she couldn't just open a Bible and read the Gospel stories. All she had in that moment was Jesus, and she chose to soak in every word he spoke. She was like the righteous man in Psalm 1, "whose delight is in the law of the LORD, and who meditates on his law day and night." She delighted in the words of Jesus. And I bet that long after Jesus left, she lay awake thinking about his teachings, replaying his words as she drifted off to sleep. His words were her life.

Being close to Jesus, resting in our identity in him, is the only thing that really matters. Nothing you do will cause him to love you more or less. My life changed when I discovered my worth does not come from the things I do or don't do. My worth is in what Jesus did for me on the cross. My identity is rooted in his Word. You can know and live in this truth too.

Coming to Christ was the beginning of a lifelong adventure, learning how he completes me. Just like Mary, after I met Jesus, I delighted in sitting at his feet. When I got married, Jesus taught me more about his love for me, the unshakable identity he's given me. As a parent, I now experience in different ways—both exciting and challenging—what it truly means to be a Mary, to rest at the Lord's feet, to seek him, to know him, and to experience him in my day-to-day life.

I've also learned the value of being a Martha, attentively caring for the needs of others around me. As I learned that both resting and using the gifts God has given me are essential parts of following Jesus, I longed to share that truth with others. That's why I started posting online and eventually launched my podcast, *Set Apart Daughters.*

This book also comes from the overflow of my heart, from the deeply rooted experience of my identity in Jesus. It's all about the heart behind our actions, and I hope that through these pages you'll discover what it means to live in your identity as one of Christ's set-apart daughters.

Before we turn to the next chapter and look at how worship sets us apart for God's purposes, I'd love to pray a blessing over you . . .

Heavenly Father, *thank you for setting us apart for your kingdom and purposes. I thank you for the gift of your Son, Jesus, and the blood he shed on the cross that sets us free from sin. I pray, Father, that you would continue to shape our identities and who you called us to be here on earth. Remind us that only Christ in us is enough and is all we need to live a righteous life in you. In Jesus's name, amen.*

2

SET APART
FOR WORSHIP

AFTER I CAME TO CHRIST, I started going regularly to my church's worship nights. I always wanted to be there! Formerly the good-time party girl, I now made church my go-to thing. I loved being in the Lord's presence and feeling so carefree. Any and every church event, you'd find me there. I just loved to praise God, and I wanted so badly to know his heart. Jesus responded with such grace, showing me more and more of his overwhelming, unfailing love.

God created us to worship. The Bible even tells us that we will be worshiping God for all eternity (see Rev. 4 for more on this). Spending time in worship draws us into deeper intimacy with God. When I worship, I feel his presence. He reminds me that I'm his daughter and he loves me. In worship, I can confidently come before my Savior, unashamed and guiltless. You can too!

When Jesus shed his blood for us, he gave us access to God as our Father. He sees no inadequacy or unworthiness in us. We can worship God and praise him, knowing he hears us. And more than that, he loves to listen to our heart's cries.

As we worship, our priorities also change. As I grew in my relationship with Jesus, the things I enjoyed changed. Who I wanted to spend time with changed. What I did with my time changed. During my first two years as a believer, when I was married with no kids and had a great deal of time to soak in God's presence, he strengthened and equipped me for the next season to come. Worship undeniably changed me, but worship does more than that. It actually changes *everything*.

What Is Worship?

Most people think of worship as singing praise to God. Worship certainly includes songs, but it goes way beyond that. At its root, worship is a heart posture, a recognition of the infinite value and majesty of God, a deliberate and joyful choice to honor him with our thoughts, words, and actions. Music can powerfully refocus our hearts as we use our mouths to glorify God, and I love to sing his praise at church . . . in my car . . . basically anywhere.

But I've also discovered that every aspect of my life can be worshipful. It's a priceless treasure to recognize that we can worship as we do dishes, have coffee with a friend, serve the needy, or change a diaper. We don't have to be singing to glorify God. Worship is first and foremost an attitude of the heart, so we can worship Jesus throughout each day. What joy that brings!

We don't simply worship because it makes us feel good, though. We worship God because he deserves it. He reigns in power. He created us. He died for us. We will never run out of reasons to worship the King of kings. In Daniel 2:20–22, the prophet gives a beautiful description of why we worship God:

> Praise be to the name of God for ever and ever;
>   wisdom and power are his.
> He changes times and seasons;
>   he deposes kings and raises up others.
> He gives wisdom to the wise
>   and knowledge to the discerning.
> He reveals deep and hidden things;
>   he knows what lies in darkness,
>   and light dwells with him.

Every single thing—*literally everything*—in the world is under the control of God. Everything! "He changes times and seasons," so every glorious sunrise and fiery sunset is the work of God. Every time the weather turns crispy or the first snowflakes fall, that's the work of God too.

"He deposes kings," meaning he controls politics. New president? God's in control. A country rises or falls? It's in God's hands. We worship and glorify God when we acknowledge him for who he truly is—almighty, all-wise, always true.

My favorite part of this passage from Daniel comes toward the end—God gives us wisdom, "and light dwells with him." God opens his truth to us every day. We just have to be watching for it. Worship enables our hearts to eagerly await and gratefully receive his wisdom.

During my first year of marriage, God taught me the wisdom of worshiping him through my daily tasks. I worked full-time at a café situated at the bottom of a massive corporate skyscraper in Oklahoma City. The café had different stations that served all kinds of food—Asian, Mexican, Italian, salad bar—you know, the works.

For the café to run smoothly, everyone had to help out with whatever needed to be done. I cashiered and did tons of other chores too. Honestly, no two days looked the same; I rarely had one specific task to do. I would prepare for breakfast and lunch, then do whatever else management assigned me for the day. Working a job like that means being ready for anything. I would take on extra assignments as needed, whether up front or in the back.

Some of those chores were fine, but some I honestly didn't want to do. At all.

One particular time, they didn't have anyone to wash dishes, so I had to fill in. I had to wash each used item by spraying it down and putting it in the industrial dishwasher, a large steel machine that filled half the room. It was gross. It smelled bad, the room was hot and steamy from the machine, and I had to pick off old pieces of food the dishwasher missed. I did not want to do it at all. While washing dishes, I realized my negative attitude.

God brought the words of Colossians 3:23–24 to my mind: "Whatever you do, work at it with all your heart, as working for the Lord, not for human masters, since you know that you will receive an inheritance from the Lord as a reward. It is the Lord Christ you are serving." *I'm sorry, Lord,* I prayed right away. *Please help me to remember that I'm working for you.*

From that day on, I kept thinking of the phrase "working for the Lord, not for human masters." If you're a believer, you work for the Lord just like I do. That concept kept me focused, giving me peace and even joy as I worked. I wasn't simply doing dishes for my boss or for customers; I was doing them for Jesus. This genuinely enabled me to do dishes with a cheerful heart. Now I didn't mind sorting the knives, forks, and spoons, drying them, making sure they were polished. Now I was motivated by faith and trust. I worked with my mind set on Scripture, thinking of the Lord. It was as if Jesus was right beside me, ministering to my spirit in what I was doing. *Whatever you do, do it for God. You're not working for man; you're working for the Lord.* That thought encouraged me and changed my perspective completely.

Working for God turned my work into worship. My actions could bring Christ honor because I did them from a heart of love, a posture of worship. I was glorifying him through my tasks, my busyness. Worshiping God as you work revives your spirit. If I had been doing dishes only to keep my boss happy or to earn that coin, I would have been annoyed and frustrated the whole time. But doing it for Jesus turned the mundane upside down. If you've never experienced this, or if like me you've forgotten that work can be worship, I encourage you to take Colossians 3 into your workplace, whether that's your home, a café, or the corporate skyrise above it. Whatever you do, keep the Lord in mind. As you worship through your work, God can use you to bless your colleagues, your family members, your neighbors. You can be used by God—and, dear sister, being used by God is an amazing feeling.

Most days at the café, I did my work quietly. When I did talk to others, though, God filled my conversations with purpose and life. I truly believe this came out of the commitment I made to worship God no matter what the task.

Jesus always gave me a word to encourage or affirm what my coworkers were doing. He consistently led me to extend a helping hand to everyone at my job.

As I worshiped and worked with my mind on Christ, something else happened. I came to realize I was working in a sea of dead people. No, not zombies. My coworkers, none of whom knew Christ, were spiritually dead. Their souls were dead, just like mine was before I met Jesus. They complained, argued, gossiped, and cursed. It was a hard atmosphere, a deadly one. In Jesus, I could bring light. And I did. God equipped me to encourage them, which was the complete opposite of what they got from other coworkers.

Some of them made fun of me and of my faith. At first I would sit with others during my breaks, but my spirit felt drained. Eventually I started sitting by myself, praying and reading the Word during my lunch break. That way God could fill me, and I could return to work from a place of worship. Spending time in the Word on break also helped me go back to work and serve my coworkers and customers well. Like I said before, worship changes *everything*.

It even changes spaces. Worship definitely doesn't take place only in a church building. Worship can happen when you're cleaning a bathroom, leading in a boardroom, wiping off a café table, parenting your child, or answering an email. Worship changes your home into a cathedral of celebration and your workplace into a palace of praise. If you and I keep our focus on Jesus, abiding in him as John 15 directs, worship is whatever we're doing.

On the other hand, anything we do from our own strength eventually exhausts us. We easily become cranky and ungrateful. We snap and gripe, even at those we love most. In our desire to do things a particular way, we can easily forget the glory of God.

I wonder if Martha thought she was doing things right when she hosted Jesus. It seems like she did. And if we read only the first few sentences of the story recorded in Luke 10, we might think so too. Mary not helping her sister might look selfish to us. Martha, the busy bee—scrubbing, cooking, cleaning, preparing for Jesus to dine with them—might look like a diligent hostess. And I'm sure she was! I honestly believe that she had a gift of hospitality. And I know from other sections of Scripture, especially John 11, that she loved Jesus.

The *things* Martha did weren't the problem; the issue lay in the heart behind her actions. The same was true for me before I learned to work from a place of worship. If you had watched my work at the café, you would have seen that I was doing the same outward actions as Martha—cleaning, doing dishes, and prepping meals. Her problem, and mine in those early days, was in the posture of our hearts. Jesus says Martha was "worried and upset about many things" (Luke 10:41). She was frustrated and anxious—my friend, I'm confident you and I can both relate to that when it comes to our work.

Just like Martha, I was tempted to work out of a wrong heart. I wanted to complain, especially in the hot dishwashing room. The enemy tempted me to resent my work. I worried that this would be my forever role, cleaning and scrubbing and prepping food. But the turnaround came when I started worshiping. Ruth Bell Graham once said, "Worship and worry cannot live in the same heart: they are mutually exclusive."[1] The first step of being free from worry is to start worshiping.

I'm so grateful that God taught me how to worship. While I outwardly did the same tasks as before, now my soul found rest. Instead of being motivated by anxiety and annoyance, God taught me to position my heart in worship, no matter what I did.

Ephesians 2:10 tells us that God has prepared in advance good works for us to do. That means we have tasks God designed for us and fitted us to do. No one else can do them! You and I have been set apart for good work; it's part of our identity in Christ. You have been gifted and equipped on purpose, for a purpose. That's why it's crucial we remember that work is not our enemy; work is not our problem. Work—whether at home, at the office, or at church—can be our place of worship. Jesus says we're missing out when we work from anxiety (see Matt. 11:28–30). Worship—*wherever* and *whenever*—is always the better way.

Worship in Every Stage

When Rashawn and I first got married and moved to Oklahoma City, we lived in a townhouse with very cheap rent. It was a big space, with three bedrooms and two and a half bathrooms, but we shared the house with roommates. We also had zero furniture. Thankfully, the landlord had left his furniture there, so we just used that.

We didn't have a bed, though, and the landlord hadn't left one behind, so we just laid our mattress on the floor. Sleeping on the ground wasn't what I imagined married life would be like. Nor was keeping our groceries in our bedroom. Since the kitchen was full of our roommates' stuff and we didn't know them very well, we turned a corner of our room into a makeshift pantry. Suffice it to say, we were not living in the lap of luxury.

I distinctly remember lying in bed one night and hearing tiny scritch-scratching sounds around me. To my shock and horror, unknown roommates of the rodent variety had moved in with us. Perhaps you can relate to my disgust in realizing that as I slept on the floor mice scampered around me. I ran to the living room, but Rashawn just laughed!

I can't believe this, I thought. *I can't believe that I moved to Oklahoma to marry a man who would let me live with mice.* I had never lived like that. I'd always had my own bed, my own stuff. My houses weren't huge, but they were clean. Sister, I felt anything but worshipful in that moment, in that space.

Rashawn and I laugh about that memory now, but during those early years, it was a big challenge to trust God and to worship him with the little we had. I learned that my contentment was found in God alone, not in where I lived or how much I earned. I decided that I would stop grumbling and worship instead. "We don't have money" turned into "In God we have all that we need." It wasn't always easy, but it was always possible. And it started with prayer.

Every morning at four or five o'clock, before we left for work, Rashawn and I went down to the bottom of the stairs, careful not to wake our roommates (except maybe the mice). There my husband and I prayed together each day before work. It was the only way to take worship with us into our workplaces.

Rashawn had given away his SUV for $500 to a former prisoner who lived across the street from us, and we were down to one little car: a two-door Hyundai Accent—little more than a go-cart, really. So much hung on that one poor car. We would drive each other to work, and somehow we made it work. In fact, because we had so little to distract us, worship was easier in some ways. During those humble beginnings, our faith felt stronger than ever. We had to depend on God for literally everything, from finances to transportation to work, making it through the day and getting back home. We understood Jesus's teaching in Matthew 18:2–4; we needed childlike faith, a son and daughter relying on our gracious heavenly Father.

In the early days of our marriage, we had little but never lacked. God always provided. We never missed a rent payment. We would randomly receive checks from former media projects or ad money. The money always came right when we needed it.

The Lord provided for us in other ways too. One time before we had kids, Rashawn was traveling to Israel and I was going to be home by myself. I really didn't want to stay home alone. I wished I could go to Puerto Rico or Florida to visit friends and family. But we earned minimum wage, and there was no way we could afford the extra trip.

At that time I was working at the café, and there was one customer I knew pretty well. He came in every day, and we chatted whenever I worked. This guy was a contractor from Texas. On Mondays he would fly into Oklahoma City for the workweek, and on Thursdays he would fly back home to Houston. Because we talked about everything and anything, I told this customer-friend about Rashawn's trip to Israel. I also told him how I wanted to visit family but couldn't afford it.

I didn't tell him with the expectation of receiving anything. It honestly never occurred to me that he'd say, "Hey,

I have a ton of airline miles. Maybe I can get you a ticket to visit your family."

"You don't have to do that," I said. "That's expensive."

"No, I'd love to do that for you," he insisted.

I could not believe God used this man to bless me in such a huge way. He graciously provided me with tickets to fly to both Florida *and* Puerto Rico, stay in each place for a few days, and then fly back to Oklahoma City. The trip lasted the same length of time that Rashawn was going to be in Israel.

Things could have gone differently, and I would have needed to trust God with that too. Depending on God doesn't always lead to getting what we hope for, but it does always lead to worshipful work. This customer saw Jesus in me, and God used his resources, in the form of accumulated frequent-flier miles, to show me that keeping my heart focused on him while using my gifts and energy—worshiping him in every situation, whether high or low—changes everything.

Working from worship is so different from the world's way of working. I wonder what would have happened if Martha had taken this trust into her work. She likely would have still served a meal to her guests that night. But as she set the table, she might have lingered in the doorway to catch a few words of Jesus's teachings. She might have stopped and listened to his conversation with Mary and even asked a few questions of her own. When we trust God's provision, we have time to rest and listen to him. The reward of worship is rest in God's provision. This is true even in the busiest and most challenging seasons of life. Motherhood is a great example.

Let the little ones . . . and their mamas . . . come to me.

Worship looks different in every stage of life. When Rashawn and I got married and were both working outside the home, I learned to worship at my job. I didn't really understand my role as a wife yet; there was hardly any time for that. I would go to work, come home, cook dinner (barely!), and wake up the next morning to do it all over again.

Once I got pregnant and complications came up in my second and third trimesters, I had to leave work. All of a sudden I was at home . . . all day, every day. *What am I supposed to be doing?* I wondered. *Just sit here and be pregnant? There has to be more.*

I couldn't see my purpose. I knew God wasn't calling me to work another eight-to-five job, though. He wanted me to do something, I sensed, but it wasn't clear yet. I decided to seek the Lord in a really focused way, reading Scripture, devouring books, watching videos, and talking with other women about their roles as godly wives and mothers. One book in particular, *The Excellent Wife* by Martha Peace, really helped me understand my purpose.

Still, I worried whether I would know what to do when Aiden arrived. Could I love him? Nurture him? Provide a safe haven for him at home? Could I love Rashawn well even as I cared for our son? No one had shown me these things, and I felt anxious about what lay ahead.

Those quiet days of worship—when I could learn from Jesus while not working outside the home—changed me. God quieted my fears and equipped me as a wife and mama. He taught me to care for Aiden, to learn and understand my role. Motherhood naturally flowed out of me, which then led me to new dimensions of worship. If God has made or ever does make you a mother, loving your child can become another avenue of worship. Again, *whatever we do*, we can do it as worship.

I loved learning to worship through caring for and loving Aiden. I did miss those uninterrupted times of sitting before God, though. Maybe you can relate. Kids are such a blessing, but they do bring a lot of chaos with them. When a baby is born, your old schedule goes out the window. You can't think about yourself like you used to.

After Aiden came, Rashawn and I were shocked to discover we now had a curfew. The baby's schedule determined a lot of what we did. We couldn't just go hang out with friends or linger at a late-night worship session or Bible study. We had to be home to put our little one to bed. And when we went on road trips or outings around the city, we had to stop and feed the baby every few hours. Honestly, a lot of hassles and stresses filled my early days of motherhood.

Virtually every first-time parent has been in this scenario: the baby starts crying, you feed him and change him, and he's still crying. It's like, "I don't know what's wrong with this child!" It was a major challenge for me to figure out how to worship with a newborn.

What does worship look like during each new stage? Finding out can be tough. I wanted to keep time with the Lord my first priority, but I didn't yet know how. And just when I started to find a rhythm of naptimes and quiet times, I got pregnant again! Now with a toddler and a baby, sitting down and really getting into the Word once again became difficult.

With each new stage, I've had to learn that worship looks different in every season. These days when I worship, I often worship with my kids. We'll go into Rashawn's office, and I'll sing as loud as I can, pouring out my heart to God. Little Aiden, our toddler, often just sits there and watches. Some days the boys fuss, and I can steal only a few moments in the secret place. But choosing to worship whenever I can, however I can, changes . . . you got it . . . *everything.*

It's amazing how God can fill us up and encourage us throughout the day as we turn to him. During this stage of my life with babies and toddlers, I don't get extended time in the Word as often as I'd like. But God is so faithful to show me new truths throughout my day, no matter what I'm doing. Whether I'm doing laundry, washing dishes, or cooking meals, he will commune with me; he will commune with you too.

As we worship, God shows us his heart for our children. We can see his tender love in creating these precious little ones. In Aiden and Eliyah's smiles, I see the face of the Lord. I see his love for me through the love I have for my boys. And I understand my own childlike dependence on God in a new way, seeing how they need me for everything. God uses different things to minister to us in each stage of life.

Watching Others Worship

By most people's standards, I'm a young mom. While a lot of women now have their first child in their thirties or even forties, I had Aiden at twenty-three. Sometimes I feel *so young* to be learning all of this. God grants so much grace, though. No matter what our age, he shows women who seek him how to be who he created us to be. As we worship, he strips off the old self and fills us with a new identity. Every day his Spirit sanctifies us.

I'm young, and I have so much more to learn about a life of worship. Maybe you're older than I am and feel the same way. There are so many ways we can grow. That's why God commands us to lean on the wisdom of older women who have learned to worship in every season of life. In the book of Titus, Paul shares the importance of having older women mentor younger women in life and worship:

> Likewise, teach the older women to be reverent in the way they live, not to be slanderers or addicted to much wine, but to teach what is good. *Then they can urge the younger women* to love their husbands and children, to be self-controlled and pure, to be busy at home, to be kind, and to be subject to their husbands, so that no one will malign the word of God. (Titus 2:3–5)

I'm so thankful for the older women in my life who have helped me. I need more of them! Throughout the book, I'll be sharing stories from mentors and friends who have encouraged me. I asked my good friend Joanna to tell how worship has impacted her in different seasons of her life:

> Every season of your life requires a different piece of you. Some seasons will be seasons of service and some will be of preparation. Some may look at a season of preparation and think, "I'm not doing enough." This is not the case! Resting at the Lord's feet restores and recharges you for seasons and assignments to come.
>
> Before God allowed me to step out into ministry, he had me in a season of resting at his feet, learning, listening, and

understanding his love and wisdom. It was a season of preparation. I was like Mary, who seated herself at the Lord's feet and was continually listening to his teaching (Luke 10:39). I would pray, read his Word, and worship him. I learned how to sit at his feet, all while rocking my babies.

I've had many encounters with the Lord, each one so different and so amazing, but there is one particular encounter of worship and prayer that changed me powerfully. In a Sunday church service, I was worshiping and praying, standing with my arms raised, hands open, and eyes closed. While praising in this way, something miraculous took place. I was standing with both feet on the ground, but my spirit began to rise up. I felt ten feet off the ground. It was like I was being pulled into God's presence. Hands still raised, eyes still closed, there I was, standing right in front of Jesus. He was the most beautiful thing my eyes have ever seen, radiating light and love.

Even though I could not see the details of his face, I sensed him smiling. I could not stop crying, but they were tears of joy. I could feel his love and joy toward me. It's like he was listening to me glorify him, yet he was listening to the prayers of my heart at the same time. He elevated my spirit for two songs, and then he slowly backed away until I could see him no longer. My spirit rejoined the earthly worship, but I was forever changed.

The only way I can think to put into words the feeling this gave me was immense joy, unlike anything I feel here on earth, in the flesh. We will not always have encounters like this, but I do believe this is exactly what's taking place every time we worship.

What a beautiful picture! Though Joanna serves in her home and at church, though she is busy in motherhood and ministry, worship is what transformed her. Worship keeps on transforming her—just like it does for me, and just like it can do for you.

God has gifted us and set us apart to do good work for his kingdom, but all of that starts with worship. The ministries we're in and the things we accomplish only matter if the posture of our heart is focused on our Lord. Jesus is so pleased with our worship, no matter what our season of life. Joanna and I both learned to abide in Jesus while caring for our newborns. Rocking, feeding, changing diapers—it all became worship.

God also gave Joanna a glimpse of the position each of us has with Christ, and I believe this can inform not only her worship but ours too. Ephesians 2:6–7 says, "And God raised us up with Christ and seated us with him in the heavenly realms in Christ Jesus, in order that in the coming ages he might show the incomparable riches of his grace, expressed in his kindness to us in Christ Jesus." When we believe in Jesus, God raises each of us up to be right beside Jesus. As Joanna experienced, he is smiling at us in love. Our spirits are always safe and secure in Jesus. Most of us won't actually get to see Jesus until we reach heaven, but what a sweet gift God gave Joanna, to get a glimpse of this ahead of time.

When we worship, we discover that we are enough through Jesus. We don't have to prove ourselves or get our worth from what we do. Our value does not come from our jobs, the size of our houses, how much money is in our bank accounts, or even how well we can take care of our kids. If we seek identity in our work, our parenting, or anything else, we'll eventually feel worthless. Purposeless. The things of earth cannot satisfy forever. We may find initial fulfillment in working without worship, but it will ultimately leave us dry.

Our worth comes only and always from our position as beloved, set-apart daughters of God.

As you do the good work God planned in advance for you to do, the goal is to keep your eyes fixed on Jesus, to abide in him. Like Martha, work with all your heart, but do so from a posture of worship. Like Mary, hang on Jesus's every word when you are able, and rest in his presence.

To close this chapter, let's worship God together in prayer:

Lord God, *we stop and worship you together right now. You are worthy of all praise, all honor, all glory. We want more of you and less of us. Help us to become women marked by rest, not hurry. By your presence and peace, not ambition and striving. By a listening ear, not a mouth that must be heard. May we, your set-apart daughters, live more-of-you-and-less-of-me lives, Lord. We love you, our Savior and King. In Jesus's name, amen.*

3

SET APART
IN PRAYER

I ALMOST BEGGED HIM to cancel.

Even though I wanted Rashawn to go to the conference, I just didn't know how I could make it through the weekend. An internal war raged in my mind. I knew God had given me everything I needed to be a mom; I knew that he would be with me. But I also had strep throat and two babies under two, and I was facing a whole weekend of caring for them by myself.

If you've never had strep throat, I'm so glad for you. It's completely miserable. Think fever, the worst sore throat you can imagine, and total exhaustion. How was I supposed to care for Aiden and Eliyah like this? Rashawn felt awful for me, but this conference was really important. We both knew God had called him to be there.

As he drove away, everything in me fought against freaking out. Panic mode wasn't going to help anyone. Anticipating all the stresses that might be would only make things worse. In my weakness, I turned to my Father.

Lord, I don't know how I'm going to do this, but I trust you to help me. I prayed the words of 2 Corinthians 12:10 back to him: *Jesus, you say that your grace is sufficient for me. I need your grace, your help, and your strength. I surrender to you.*

His peace wrapped around me like a warm blanket. My strep throat wasn't miraculously cured, but I felt strengthened. The weekend no longer looked completely impossible.

Did the boys and I have a sent-from-heaven couple of days? Not exactly. I vividly remember nursing four-month-old Eliyah while chasing after Aiden, who was screaming at the top of his lungs because I told him he couldn't eat toothpaste from the tube clutched in his little toddler hands. When he found out toothpaste wasn't on the menu, Aiden turned his attention to eating deodorant. (What?!) Another tantrum erupted when I took that away too. But even in these difficulties, I felt God carrying me in his loving arms.

Mothering is challenging in the best of circumstances. Trying to figure out what your children need or why on earth they're doing what they're doing when you're sick and on your own because a spouse is traveling (or perhaps because you're a single parent) feels downright overwhelming. Can I get an amen?

Beloved daughter, whether or not you're a mama, I know you've encountered circumstances that feel altogether too much for you. The process of maturing into the women God wants us to be can be hard. Growing is painful; we can't carry the weight of it. That's why Jesus invites us to cast all our cares on him (1 Pet. 5:7). God's shoulders are way broader than ours. He's our loving heavenly Father, so much stronger than us and so ready to help us, his precious daughters.

God has called me to the work of mothering. It's an amazing and difficult calling. Honestly, I fail every day. At times I don't know how I'm going to care for these little disciples for the next eighteen years. Sometimes I wonder, *Can I do this without losing my mind?* My goal every single day is to honor God, to please him. How can I do that when I mess up so often?

I have found the answer in working from a place of prayer, a place of surrender to Jesus. When I try to work from any other place, things fall apart. When I work from a place of prayer—as a mom, in serving the needy, as a hostess, or as an employee—I experience God's strength and sustaining power. And I want that for you too.

What's Eating You?

When I think of Martha, striving to impress her guests, assuming that what she was doing wasn't enough, I think of the times when I've become overwhelmed with self-doubt. *Am I doing enough? Are my kids taken care of? Does my husband feel loved? Am I where God wants me to be?*

These kinds of thoughts eat at many of us, don't they? I imagine they ate at Martha. But the only way to cast off that self-doubt is to lay those fears and worries at the feet of Jesus.

It's tempting to look at Luke 10:38–42 and assume that Mary didn't struggle with doubt. We assume that she sat at the feet of Jesus completely at rest and confident. But Mary was only human. While she may have been in the right place that evening, I'm sure there were times when she let fear and doubt control her. Did she wonder if she was spending enough time caring for others? Did she wonder if her sister looked down on her for not serving in the same way? I wonder if she doubted whether she was giving enough, encouraging enough, listening enough.

Self-doubt and prayer can't exist at the same moment. If our minds are fixed on Jesus, our self-doubt has to bow to his authority. On the other hand, when our minds are filled with worries and insecurity, we cannot experience his peace and work from a place of strength and surrender. I know which I prefer—what about you?

A passage from the book of Philippians has transformed my experience with prayer. I believe it can do the same for you. The apostle Paul writes, "Don't worry about anything; instead, pray about everything. Tell God what you need, and thank him for all he has done. Then you will experience God's peace, which exceeds anything we can understand. His peace will guard your hearts and minds as you live in Christ Jesus" (Phil. 4:6–7 NLT).

When you first look at these verses, it might be hard to imagine not worrying about *anything*. But Paul tells us the reason we can do this is that we have a choice. We can choose where to fix our minds. Instead of worrying and doubting, we can turn our attention to prayer, telling God what we need and thanking him for all he's done. A life-changing promise comes with this passage: "Then you will experience God's peace, which exceeds anything we can understand."

Isn't that exactly what we need as women—a peace that goes beyond us, a peace that's not dependent on how well we perform, how gifted we are, how important our work is, or how often we succeed? I have personally experienced what it's like to have Christ Jesus guard my heart and my mind. It changes *everything*.

Philippians 4:6–7 teaches us to pray by acknowledging our needs to God and giving thanks. These are an inseparable pair, like two sides of the same coin. A prayer of petition (asking) is incomplete without praise and thanksgiving. I know how challenging it can be to give thanks when you're in the middle of a fierce storm—a cancer diagnosis, the loss of a job, being rejected by a friend or family member.

In these moments we may not be able to thank God for the circumstances, but I have learned that we can always be thankful for God's character. He has been faithful in the past, he is faithful right now, and he will be faithful forever. That's what his Word teaches, and that's something we can be thankful for no matter what's going on in our daily lives.

Praying in the way Philippians 4 describes may feel natural to you, or you may feel lost or confused. So many people fear that they don't know how to pray. Very few of us are taught to pray in the same way we're taught math or the alphabet. I'd love to share a bit of my journey, hoping that it can help you learn to work from the place of peace and strength that prayer makes possible.

From Repeat to Release

As a child, I attended the Catholic church with my grandparents. My grandfather served as one of the priests at our local parish, and religion is considered very important in Puerto Rico. I remember my grandmother teaching me a small prayer that I devotedly recited every single night before bed. I also learned the Lord's Prayer.

While there are so many wonderful truths in the Lord's Prayer and in the Bible teachings that I heard while attending mass, I did not encounter Jesus in the repetitious prayers that I prayed or the religious services I attended throughout childhood. It wasn't until I turned twenty that I began to meet Jesus in prayer.

In the dead of night, sitting in my car and desperate for help, I cried out to Jesus on my own for the first time. I didn't use fancy words. I don't even remember exactly what I said. I only know my heart was reaching out in a real way. For a while before this, I had been listening to people pray at the Bible study I attended. Their prayers were authentic, straight from the heart. I had never imagined I could talk to God that way. But that experience of praying in my car at three in the morning felt like being released from a prison of self-doubt, worry, and bitterness.

I went from praying repetitive religious prayers to praying personal and intimate prayers to my heavenly Father. I continued to learn about prayer from the godly men and women around me, listening to them pray and leaning into the same kind of prayers. One of the best ways God's daughters can learn to pray is by surrounding themselves with praying people. If you feel unsure in your prayer life, join a prayer group. Listen to the prayers of godly people. This can be such a great way to start praying on your own.

I also learned a great deal about prayer by reading the Word of God. Some people overlook this aspect of prayer, but it's been so helpful for me as I seek to work from a place of prayer rather than a place of drivenness. I can't always come up with the right words. I don't always know what's best for myself or the people I love. But when I pray God's Word back to him, I align myself with his will and his plan. Praying his Word is praying with power.

Spending time reading the Psalms in particular helped me learn to pray and really strengthened my prayer life. For example, I can pray Psalm 17 with confidence because God himself wrote these words through David: "I am praying to you because I know you will answer, O God. Bend down and listen as I pray. Show me your unfailing love in wonderful ways" (Ps. 17:6–7 NLT).

Learning to pray God's Word is an amazing weapon in the spiritual battles we face as we seek to leave behind self-doubt, worry, and insecurity. The world is always telling us we're not enough, but when we pray God's Word, we pray with power and confidence in our identity as beloved daughters. "Put on salvation as your helmet, and take the sword of the Spirit, which is the word of God," Paul commands us in Ephesians 6. "Pray in the Spirit at all times and on every occasion. Stay alert and be persistent in your prayers for all believers everywhere" (Eph. 6:17–18 NLT). The Word of God is the only offensive weapon in our spiritual armor—an undefeatable sword! I continue learning how to pray Scripture, and I urge you to do the same.

I also want to invite you to learn another kind of prayer that will enable you to work from a place of peace and strength rather than fear and doubt. The prayer of surrender is a challenging one to learn but is so important for us as God's set-apart daughters.

At Jesus's Feet

By sitting at Jesus's feet as we see her doing in Luke 10, Mary assumed a position of humility and surrender before the Lord. Sitting in that way meant she could not do anything else. She trusted that what she was doing in that moment was enough. And it was.

Humility and surrender aren't very popular words for women in our day and age. For many women, those words indicate weakness or being used as a doormat. According to God's Word, however, that couldn't be further from the truth. Consider how the Bible describes the humility of our Savior Jesus in this powerful passage:

> Don't be selfish; don't try to impress others. Be humble, thinking of others as better than yourselves. Don't look out only for your own interests, but take an interest in others, too.

> You must have the same attitude that Christ Jesus had.

> > Though he was God,
> > > he did not think of equality with God
> > > as something to cling to.
> > Instead, he gave up his divine privileges;
> > > he took the humble position of a slave
> > > and was born as a human being.
> > When he appeared in human form,
> > > he humbled himself in obedience to God
> > > and died a criminal's death on a cross. (Phil. 2:3–8 NLT)

When we work from a place of self-doubt, it's often because we're trying to impress other people. Working from a place of worry can make us selfish; we have to figure out how to control things to feel less anxious, which can lead us to put our needs above the needs of others. As the passage above revealed, this is the exact opposite of what Jesus did.

In order to follow Jesus's example of humility, we must learn to surrender, and surrender happens in prayer.

I learned surrender in a very painful way years ago. As I mentioned earlier, I had only been in the United States a short time when I was thrown into high school with a gigantic language barrier. To that point I had always been an A or B student, but all of a sudden I couldn't comprehend what I was being taught. My English skills weren't enough to keep pace with the subjects in my Florida high school.

As my senior year finished and graduation approached, I looked through lists of colleges and universities. I dreamed of following in my dad's footsteps. He had both a bachelor's and master's degree. I wanted to be a successful woman. I wanted to make him proud. To make my college dream a reality, I needed to pass a test that would show my competency in English. I studied so hard for that test. I spent so much money on tutoring. I did my best.

And I didn't pass.

As I mentioned before, I received a completion certificate for finishing high school, but because I did not pass this test, I could not get an official diploma that would have allowed me to attend college. I was completely shattered. I was embittered and angry at the world. I couldn't understand. Feelings of failure, self-doubt, worry, and confusion suffocated me day and night. I had no idea what I was supposed to do with my life, so I fell into a depression and began making a lot of really bad choices.

But God had a much bigger plan for my life.

I don't know what would have happened if I had gone to college, but I do know what actually happened as a result of my dream being shattered: I met Jesus. I learned to surrender to his will for my life. Remember that prayer I prayed in my car at three o'clock in the morning? That was a prayer of total surrender that came from my broken heart: *I can't do this on my own, Jesus. I need you.*

I didn't understand how powerful the prayer of surrender was in fighting self-doubt, worry, and insecurity until God started to unwind my heart from the fears and doubts. But as time went on, I could trace back to that prayer of surrender and see the freedom and new life he was giving me. My work—my whole life—changed. I was no longer working to prove myself or to settle the question of whether I was good enough. I was working from a place of prayer, surrendered to God.

There were times when the old insecurities tried to creep back into my mind. The enemy is a liar, and he tried telling me lies: *You couldn't even pass that test. You're nothing without a degree.* Learning my identity as God's beloved daughter and knowing his unique plan for my life helped me reject these lies and replace them with God's truth.

One of my absolute favorite verses in fighting the lie of "not good enough" is Philippians 1:6: "And I am certain that God, who began the good work within you, will continue his work until it is finally finished on the day when Christ Jesus returns" (NLT). It's not my work that matters; it's the work God is doing in me. Surrendering to that work is the pathway to peace and power. Knowing that God *will* finish his good work in me gives me everything I need to live for his glory.

The Word of God gives us wonderful prayers of surrender that we can pray back to God. With Jesus we can pray, "Not my will, but yours be done" (Luke 22:42) and "May your Kingdom come soon. May your will be done on earth, as it is in heaven" (Matt. 6:10 NLT). We can also pray, "O Sovereign LORD! You made the heavens and earth by your strong hand and powerful arm. Nothing is too hard for you!" (Jer. 32:17 NLT).

I continue to learn how to work and serve from a place of prayerful surrender. I pray you will too. As we do, we'll be able to sit at Jesus's feet, peaceful and confident that we don't have to work harder or pretend to be someone we're not to please him . . . or anyone else for that matter! Whatever you're facing, remember that nothing is too hard for God. May his will be done in your life as it is in heaven, and may you learn to run to your heavenly Father as the beloved daughter you are.

Daddy-Daughter Time

If Aiden or Eliyah ran into the room right now and asked me for a glass of water, I would get it for them. They can't do it on their own. If they fell and skinned their knees, I would quickly bandage their little legs. There's nothing I wouldn't do for my boys if they were in need. That's the heart our heavenly Father has for us too.

That's why when Jesus says to his stressed-out daughter, "My dear Martha, you are worried and upset over all these details! There is only one thing worth being concerned about" (Luke 10:41–42 NLT), I don't think we should hear only scolding in his voice. Jesus loved Martha. The Bible makes that absolutely clear in John 11:5: "Now Jesus loved Martha and her sister and Lazarus." It doesn't get more straightforward than that. In Luke 10, he was simply inviting her to work from a place of peace and surrender as his beloved daughter rather than striving and struggling as a woman who had to prove herself.

My friend, sometimes I feel so helpless and weak. I cannot depend on my own strength. I need God, and through prayer I rely on his never-failing strength. I have to rely on him 24/7! When I'm in the midst of anxiety and frustration, I often struggle to submit to the Lord in prayer. I admit it—sometimes prayer becomes my last option when emotions and feelings overtake me. But running to my heavenly Father as his beloved daughter is always best. When prayer is our first response to any given situation, our perspective shifts off our problems and back onto God's promises.

A beloved earthly daughter feels at home in her father's house. When we trust our heavenly Father, we pray from a place of "at home-ness." The Bible has a special word for this: *abiding*. We work and serve best when we prayerfully make our hearts at home in Jesus and allow the Holy Spirit to make his home in us. When I pray as a daughter, I know that I'm secure and safe; my life is hidden in Christ, just like Colossians 3:3 promises. Passages like John 15:7–17 and 1 John 4 have also helped me learn the abiding aspect of prayer.

Praying as a daughter helps me to enjoy God. It draws me deeper into my friendship with Jesus, and it helps me to share with him the good things happening in my life as well as the things I often struggle with—negative attitudes, procrastination, lack of patience, anger, and even messy thoughts from my past.

Prayer is a very special Daddy-daughter time. And working from this kind of prayer enables us to delight in our progression as set-apart, beloved children. Serving from abiding prayer reminds us how God's grace is constantly shaping and molding us into the women he calls us to be—lights for Christ in a chaotic, dark world.

Instead of working from a place of self-doubt, let's press into our identity as beloved daughters. The apostle John writes, "See how very much our Father loves us, for he calls us his children, and that is what we are!" (1 John 3:1 NLT). That is who you are, sister. Pray from that place and watch everything change.

From the Overflow

As we bring this chapter to a close, I want to share a great example of prayerful service with you. Tanda, my friend and sister in Christ, so powerfully displays the aspects of praying from a place of surrender, praying as a beloved daughter, and praying God's Word. I just wish you could know Tanda. She is truly amazing!

Tanda and her husband recently faced a major challenge in their home life. Their family devotions had become a box to be checked off, and Tanda could see that even though her kids had made professions of faith, their relationship with Jesus had taken a back seat to doing good things for God and knowing the right Bible answers. Needless to say, Tanda felt discouraged and wondered if she had somehow failed as a mom.

One evening, God spoke to my friend. Jesus invited Tanda to surrender her family's devotional time to him. He wanted her to do the work of mothering and to serve her family from a place of prayer, not of self-doubt, worry, and insecurity. The Holy Spirit wanted her to leave room for him to act instead of trying to control the circumstances herself. God wanted Tanda to remember that he is working *all* things together for the good of those who are called according to his purpose (Rom. 8:28). He is the faithful one; he will complete the good work he started in her children (Phil. 1:6).

In response to God's invitation to do things differently, Tanda and her husband prayed together as a son and daughter dearly loved by their heavenly Father. They humbly surrendered to Jesus, thanking him for all he's done and prayerfully acknowledging their need for his help. Amazingly, when Tanda gave up having to control things, her kids' hearts began to change. The Holy Spirit led their family to deeper dependence on him. They began to listen together for the Spirit's voice. They spoke life to one another. They worshiped together.

When Tanda gave her self-doubt and worries to God, he came through in incredible ways. Tanda went from feeling like a failure as a mom and spiritual leader to being able to work and serve as an empowered daughter. Spirit-led prayer made the difference.

Prayer transforms us from doubtful worriers into women who can remain at the feet of Jesus with peace and confidence. It takes us from doubting whether we're enough to giving those doubts over to the only One whose opinion matters. And it also comes with an amazing added benefit: out of the overflow of our prayers of surrender and trust as daughters of the King, others' lives are changed. Tanda's family was changed by the prayers of her and her husband. Prayer transformed her work and service as a mom. My work and my family are changed by the prayers I humbly pray. How you work, how you serve, and who you are will be changed by prayer too, as will the lives of those around you. I invite you to pray with me as we close this chapter.

Heavenly Father, *thank you for loving us with an everlasting love. Thank you for making us your daughters through the death and resurrection of your Son, Jesus. Holy Spirit, thank you for helping us, comforting us, convicting us of sin, and leading us in your truth. Please release us from the chains of self-doubt, worry, and insecurity. May we learn to work and serve from a place of prayer, Lord. And may we grow in joy and love as we do this, empowered by you. In Jesus's name, amen.*

4

SET APART
FROM COMPARISON

GOD GAVE ME A GIFT that was difficult for me to accept as a child. In a sea of perfectly straight-haired Puerto Rican girls, my hair felt chaotically curly, not beautifully unique. I used to tie my hair in a ponytail as slick as you can possibly imagine. I hated my curls, didn't want anyone to see my "real" hair, and learned every style that would conceal what God had given me. I wanted to be like everyone but myself.

The other girls at my private Puerto Rican school seemed to have way more than I did. Some had beautiful makeup, and some dressed in super nice outfits. Seeing them—all day, every day—led me to believe I needed to look like them in order to be accepted. I started applying makeup, but my first attempts were complete fails. I showed up at school with makeup but still felt totally "other" and embarrassed because I just couldn't get the look my group of school friends had. I never felt comfortable in my own skin.

Truthfully, growing up apart from Christ was uncomfortable in a lot of ways. Every circle I joined, including friends and family, overflowed with criticism, gossip, and dirty joking. I so often felt afraid of being who I was, because I didn't want to be made fun of or judged. In order to fit in and be cool, I would often "put on" different personalities. I became the Denisse who was down for anything and everything, the Denisse who knew what she wanted in life, or the Denisse who didn't put up with people's insults. I never felt secure or safe, because I was always changing myself based on who I was with, how I felt around them, and what I thought they wanted from me. It was beyond uncomfortable; it was completely exhausting.

When Jesus rescued me, my relationships changed dramatically. It brought me such joy to be myself and feel accepted, to be loved no matter where I came from, what I had, or where I might be headed. I relished the freedom that gave me. Maybe that's why it surprised me when I started to struggle with comparing myself to other Christian sisters.

Over the years, I've been tempted to compare myself with the outgoing, perfectly put-together Christian woman everyone loves. Or to the woman who's so brilliant in the kitchen that every meal is Insta post-worthy. Or the woman who never seems to fight with or disrespect her husband. And what about the mom who knows exactly how to parent toddlers? You know, the mama with neatly labeled sensory bins who understands things like developing gross motor skills. How do I compare myself with her and not feel like a total failure?

Anyone else ever felt like you're drowning in a sea of comparison, even with Christian sisters you love? I don't want that! I want to celebrate what God's given others, not feel less-than because of it.

I've even battled the "not enough" lie in comparing myself to Rashawn. My husband does so many incredible things for God; I honestly don't know how he keeps up with everything the Lord puts on his plate. After we first got married, Rashawn often traveled to influencer events and conferences, on mission trips and evangelistic outreaches. From Oklahoma to Los Angeles, the Philippines to Israel, Rashawn always seemed on mission. Because I couldn't travel with him on many of these trips, I'd stay home by myself, feeling totally unimportant. It was so difficult for me to separate my identity in Christ—I am so important to my Savior—from my identity as the wife of a VIP influencer.

I share the messy details of my journey with you to set the stage for where we're headed in this chapter . . . a place that's super personal and may be super painful for some of us. As you can see, I've played the comparison game all too often in my life. I imagine a lot of us have. Thankfully, we can find hope and freedom in hearing what God has to say about comparison, understanding our unique gifted-ness, and owning it with peace and joy in Jesus. Let's start by looking at comparison through a biblical lens.

From Microscope to Telescope

Lots of books, articles, and blogs have been written about the story of Mary and Martha in Luke 10. I've also heard plenty of sermons and podcasts about these sisters. Most come to one conclusion: *We should all try to be like Mary.* I can absolutely see why this point is emphasized again and again.

A curious thing happens to many women who hear this message, though. Those of us who are task-oriented, those of us who are business-minded, those of us who are creative, those of us who are warriors—we feel like there's something irredeemably wrong with us. We compare ourselves with Mary and feel seriously *not enough.*

But this game of comparison is not what Jesus intended. One set of giftings isn't more valuable or honoring to him than another. He was simply pointing out how in that moment Mary was operating from a position of peace—*I am enough*—while Martha, in all her exaggerated busyness, was operating from a position of striving—*I am not enough.*

Instead of being drawn to sit at the feet of Jesus, many of us feel like we're competing with Mary, our sister in Christ. We assume she must have always gotten things right, but as I've pointed out before, Mary was only human. Comparing ourselves to any woman in one isolated moment of her life can make us feel less than and not enough.

Nineteenth-century author Josh Billings once wrote, "Love looks through a telescope; envy, through a microscope."[1] We often take a microscopic—and loveless— approach to the story of Mary and Martha. We envy Mary and condemn Martha. But that's not the point of this story.

Jesus is the point.

I want us to turn a telescopic glance back at Luke 10:38– 42 and see Jesus's love for both of these sisters. Christ wasn't exalting Mary above her sister (or any of us). Rather, he was inviting Martha to be at peace. Mary had chosen peace in that moment, but Jesus wasn't encouraging Martha to competitive comparison. He was inviting her to observe an example and follow. He's inviting us to follow that example too.

All Bad?

Women seem as prone to comparison as fish are to swimming. Is there any way we can simply stop comparing? This may surprise you, but I don't think so. However, I do think there's a way to shift the energy we often bend toward unhealthy and dishonoring comparison in a better and God-honoring direction. Before we get to the good news behind that, let's sift through a bit of bad news.

This probably won't come as a shock to you, but comparing ourselves to other women robs us of joy, peace, and confidence. You and I know this at the core of who we are; we can *feel* it. Proverbs 14:30 tells us clearly, "A heart at peace gives life to the body, but envy rots the bones." When we compare and compete with our sisters in Christ, we poison the water in which we swim together. You and I both know the rotten feeling that wells up inside when we compare ourselves to others and feel less than and not enough.

On the simplest level, to compare means "to examine (two or more objects, ideas, people, etc.) in order to note similarities and differences."[2] That doesn't sound all bad. What actually poisons us as women are the thoughts behind comparison, the belief that there's an automatic ranking system associated with this examination—one must be better, one worse. Ultimately, that's the bad news: toxic comparison makes us competitors for first place in whatever category we consider important, whether that's physical appearance, spiritual maturity, financial security, parenting, or something else. We look at our giftedness and think *not enough*, which is not only bad news but also a poisonous lie!

Now to the good news: this is not how Jesus sees us as his body. We are not competitors for his approval or for first place among our sisters. And there's another dynamic to this good news: we can turn the energy we may have previously used for unhealthy comparison to help us grow spiritually.

The Bible commands us to be imitators of God. "Follow God's example, therefore, as dearly loved children, and walk in the way of love, just as Christ loved us and gave himself up for us as a fragrant offering and sacrifice to God" (Eph. 5:1–2). We are called to look to Jesus, examine whether our life looks like his, and make changes empowered by his Holy Spirit. This is a process of comparison, but it's not a comparison game, a comparison trap, or a competition.

I compare my life with Christ's and know that I don't measure up; this makes me sad, but it doesn't make me envious. The kind of sorrow I experience when convicted by sin doesn't lead to shame or fear but to life. The Bible clearly says, "Godly sorrow brings repentance that leads to salvation and leaves no regret, but worldly sorrow brings death" (2 Cor. 7:10). Worldly comparison poisons us, but comparing our lives to Jesus and letting God the Holy Spirit transform us "into his image with ever-increasing glory" (2 Cor. 3:18) causes us to mature spiritually and experience more of the abundant life Christ died to give us (see John 10:10).

Okay, deep breath here, sister. I know this is complex. But it's so essential that we take our eyes off one another as competitors and fix our eyes on Jesus, who loves us and sets a perfect example for us to follow. In order to follow this example, I must compare two different things: my life and

Christ's life. The same is true for you. Of course, this is only possible by God's grace. Otherwise we'd quickly fall into complete despair. But when we choose to examine Jesus's life and make changes in our own life to become more like him, we live more deeply, truly, and freely.

As we earnestly seek God, we can also look to the example of older, godlier women, sisters who spur us on to love and good deeds, like Hebrews 10:24 encourages. The Bible tells us to follow the example of Jesus *and* to deliberately seek out mentoring from those who have walked with Christ more intimately. Paul told the Corinthian church, "Follow my example, as I follow the example of Christ" (1 Cor. 11:1).

This means we can grow by examining the lives of godly Christians and following the patterns we see. This involves comparison—examining two things and noting similarities and differences—but it takes competition completely out of the process. When we look at a godly woman and compare our life to hers, it can infuse us with holy longing to be more like Jesus or it can lead us to compete with our sister. Toxic comparison can, of course, also lead us to feel ashamed that we're not as good as she is or to despair that we'll never have the kind of walk with Jesus that she has. But again, the poison is not from the process of observing differences; it comes when we rank ourselves as if one were better and another worse.

I know it's difficult to imagine how you could move from comparing as a competition to the kind of comparison that enables us to grow in Christ with joy and holy longing, but this is a worthy goal, isn't it? Instead of investing so much energy looking at others and seeing how we stack up to them, what if we diligently followed the examples of Jesus and of godly women who follow him?

Don't you think that might lead to something good?

If you're having a tough time imagining this, let me share a couple stories from my life that helped me move beyond the comparison trap and toward deeper trust in Jesus.

Unexpected

Right after Rashawn and I got married, we lived in a tiny house. And this was before tiny houses were popular and chic! The seven hundred square feet we lived in felt like enough for the two of us (most of the time . . . ha-ha!), but we also wanted to open our house to family and friends. I was really bummed that when the time came to host a potluck or any gathering in our home, I could invite only a few people without making everyone feel like Vienna sausages in a can.

I felt like my tiny house wasn't good enough. Hospitality is one of my main giftings from the Lord. I wanted to honor him by hosting people for a warm meal and fellowship, but I only had so much space. I instantly began to feel discouraged and self-conscious, wondering what others would say about me, whether some people would wonder why they weren't invited, or what would happen if I invited too many. What if people didn't have a comfortable place to sit? What if, instead of feeling at peace in our home, people felt claustrophobic? I looked at other people's houses and thought, *I could definitely serve the Lord better with a bigger home.* This honestly plagued me.

Thankfully, God guided me away from such toxic thinking. He works in mysterious and beautiful ways when we step outside our fears of not being enough, when we say no to competing with other sisters in Christ. He gently reminded me that everything he's given me comes from his hand; that means it *is* enough! He's the God who turned one little boy's loaves and fish into lunch and leftovers for thousands of people. My tiny house wasn't an issue to Jesus. God knows everything, so I can trust him with invitations and space issues just like I trust him with everything else.

It wasn't always easy to stop comparing my little space to the houses of my sisters in Christ. But when I courageously stopped competing and instead learned from godly women who showed me hospitality and modeled opening their homes for the sake of Christ, I grew so much.

As I determined to follow the example of hospitality even in my tiny house, amazing and unexpected things happened. A brother in the Lord who has suffered some terrible struggles once described coming through our doors like traveling to a different country. He felt welcome, safe, loved, and accepted with us. I had never heard anything like that! His words bless me every time I remember them. Many of us couldn't imagine the day-to-day things this man had faced. How precious it was that we could love him in Jesus's name. When we open our homes and allow the Lord to create spaces of healing and safety for the weary and hurting, joy overflows for everyone.

What if I had been too ashamed of our house to open the doors to others? What if I had let the comparison game ruin any chance for Rashawn and me to be used by the Lord? I'm so grateful Jesus helped us make our home a place that his presence can fill and where life change can begin.

The unexpected blessing of stepping outside of comparison and following the example set by Jesus as his beloved, set-apart daughter is that what we have and what we do is *always enough* in his hands.

Hospitality may not be your primary gifting. Each of us is unique. God set you apart for his purposes, and those purposes will be different from mine. The key is to own the gifts God gives you without falling into the trap of toxic comparison and competition. Instead, follow the example of Jesus—whether your gift is encouragement or truth-telling, worship through music or teaching, showing mercy or prayer. Then, without a spirit of competition, follow the example of godly Christians around you who are gifted in similar ways. This leads to the peaceful and joyful use of God's gifts, even when it means growing and stretching in new ways.

Beans, Rice, and Jesus Christ

I could eat Puerto Rican chicken, beans, rice, and plantains all day, every day. I grew up doing that very thing! I couldn't imagine life any other way. Funny thing, though: not only could Rashawn *imagine* eating other things—he also *wanted* to. My husband grew up with an entirely different menu than I did. And even though he enjoyed my Puerto Rican cooking, he did ask whether I'd be willing to make some of the dishes he loved. Trouble was, I had no idea how to cook anything but the foods I had grown up making.

Again, the feelings of being less than and not enough threatened me. I looked at other women, with all the organic products in their pantries and gourmet-looking meals on their social media feeds, and I felt totally discouraged. I'm not going to lie—for a time I allowed that comparison to fuel competition in me. Nothing good came of that. Shame and fear are the results of toxic comparison.

I'm so thankful for our tenderhearted, gracious God, who once again reminded me that in him, I am already enough. I may not have known how to cook the things Rashawn loves, but guess what—I could learn. Instead of being fueled by fear and shame that I wasn't good enough, especially compared to other wives I knew, I focused my energies on loving my husband the way God calls me to love him, the way modeled by my godly sisters in Christ.

I love the passage in Titus 2 that calls older women to "urge the younger women to love their husbands and children, to be self-controlled and pure, to be busy at home, to be kind, and to be subject to their husbands, so that no one will malign the word of God" (vv. 4–5). The mentor sisters around me encouraged me to love my husband and be busy at home. I could learn to cook some new things, not because I was competing with other women but because I love my husband and can use my energy (be busy) at home in a God-honoring way. I saw how older women I respected did this, and it encouraged me to grow as a wife and mom. I didn't need to *be* them. Instead, I could joyfully follow their example as they followed Jesus.

Having immigrated to the United States as a teenager, I've often felt different from the women around me, and in many ways I'll always be Puerto Rican at heart. Being different felt so scary for the curly-haired-child me and the newly married I'm-not-as-important-as-my-influential-husband me.

Praise God that being different is celebrated in the body of Christ, and today I celebrate my unique role as part of that body.

This isn't my idea; it comes straight from Scripture. The apostle Paul writes,

> Just as a body, though one, has many parts, but all its many parts form one body, so it is with Christ. . . .
>
> Now if the foot should say, "Because I am not a hand, I do not belong to the body," it would not for that reason stop being part of the body. And if the ear should say, "Because I am not an eye, I do not belong to the body," it would not for that reason stop being part of the body. If the whole body were an eye, where would the sense of hearing be? If the whole body were an ear, where would the sense of smell be? But in fact God has placed the parts in the body, every one of them, just as he wanted them to be. If they were all one part, where would the body be? (1 Cor. 12:12, 15–19)

Every part of the body matters, and every sister in Christ matters. We are not all the same—thank God for that! We each have unique and special roles to play. We can watch the way others do things and be spurred on to love and good deeds rather than competition. We have better things to do in life than allowing toxic shame and fear to lead us into the comparison game.

When we compare in unhealthy ways, we look at others through the filter of our weaknesses. To make matters worse, we then look at ourselves through the filter of others' strengths. What a mess! We need to reject these filters completely. May God give all of us eyes to see our own strengths and weaknesses in the light of his grace and sufficiency. Join me in living a truly unfiltered life by celebrating our differences and refusing to compete and compare.

God gave me two sisters in Christ—Jasmyne and Christy—who exemplify very different callings and unique giftedness. If I let myself compare my life to theirs in an unhealthy way, I could easily feel less than. Instead, their examples draw me closer to Jesus. As we close this chapter, let me share a bit about them and encourage you to learn from their example of following Christ.

Mary and Martha . . . at Their Best

God created Jasmyne with incredible energy and discipline. She's also one of the most selfless people I know. She always goes above and beyond when it comes to serving and filling a need. One time when I got sick, she offered (without my asking!) to come over and help me with the kids, clean the house, and bring dinner. That day she greeted me with a delicious bowl of chicken tortilla soup. As I took a desperately needed nap, Jasmyne began to organize the house and clean the kitchen. And when I say "clean," I want you to understand something about Jasmyne—she sees what others don't when it comes to cleaning. She scrubs away every food stain and every bit of hidden grime. This woman cleans for the glory of God!

I know this because I asked her why she cleans the way she does. She gently responded that it was therapeutic for her; she could worship and rest while she cleaned. Wow! That's not like most of us who deep clean only when we're frustrated or angry. Jasmyne enjoys what she does and finds God in the midst of it. She loves caring for others' needs.

She sees a need and fills it, whether she's asked to or not. God uses her so powerfully.

My other friend, Christy, does not have the kind of physical energy that Jasmyne has. Rapidly advancing multiple sclerosis landed Christy in a wheelchair a couple years ago. Some days she can't even transfer from her bed to her chariot (her husband's affectionate term for Christy's wheelchair). Christy and her pastor-husband ministered together in powerful ways and raised five amazing children prior to her diagnosis.

It would be so easy for Christy to feel sorry for herself, to compare herself to a woman like Jasmyne or even to the way she used to be before MS. Christy lives above that, though. She would, of course, want you to know that she's not perfect; there are days of emotional, physical, and spiritual struggle. But I just wish you could see the light of the Lord in my sister Christy.

Christy finds herself at the feet of Jesus 24/7, whether she's at the hospital, in bed, or praying with her husband. She's learned to embrace the gift of truly being at the feet of Jesus without comparing herself to other women who are more physically able. To the watching world her joy is unexplainable, but we in the body of Christ know it comes from the fullness of his Spirit. She encourages everyone she meets. Being wheelchair-bound does not stop her from worshiping Jesus. No matter her outward circumstances, Christy's worshipful life overflows in blessing to others.

Looking at Christy and Jasmyne makes me think beyond the story in Luke 10 to celebrate Mary and Martha at their best. Christy's life is very much one of sitting at the feet of Jesus in worship and blessing countless people through that. Jasmyne is active and is always serving, often behind the scenes and in the kitchen. Though Martha may have felt frustrated and not enough in the moment Luke records, at other times I believe that she served from a place of rest and confidence like Jasmyne does.

Such different sisters . . . such amazing sisters. I look at their lives and want to grow like they do. I don't want to compete with them. I don't feel less than when I'm around them. They aren't competing with me, and I'm not trying to one-up them.

There is such joy when we finally understand that we are enough in Jesus because he is always enough in us and through us. Please allow me to seal that truth in you with a prayer of blessing:

Lord Jesus, *you know everything about us. You know how hard it is for us not to compare ourselves in toxic ways. Holy Spirit, please break every chain of unhealthy comparison and any feelings of not being good enough that would steal our joy and fuel our sin. We confess our complete dependence on you to change us from the inside out. We worship you, our beloved and holy Savior, our perfect example. May the truth of your Word go deep within us, and may it be sealed in our hearts by you, Holy Spirit, so that we can serve and love without poisonous comparison. It's for your glory that we live and work. May our gifts be used for your honor. In Jesus's name, amen.*

5

SET APART
FROM APPROVAL-SEEKING

No matter how many things I checked off my to-do list, it just kept getting longer.

My sweet Aiden was turning two in just a few days, and my dad was flying in to celebrate with us. I wanted the house to be spotless and to smell amazing. I wanted the guest room to be cozy and comfortable. I wanted our car to be free—just for a few days—of the crumbs, toys, toddler socks, and miscellaneous diaper-changing necessities that seem to multiply in any vehicle I drive. And I wanted to make sure nothing was broken. My super handy dad always finds something that needs fixing. I hate that! I wanted him to relax at our house, not do construction.

Basically, I wanted everything to be perfect.

I know, I know—I'm not supposed to want that.

I'm supposed to be okay with the messiness of life and embrace the grace of Jesus no matter what tumbles out of my car when the doors fly open. But being totally honest, my friend, I really wanted things to be perfect for my dad's visit.

I've always been a daddy's girl. What Dad thought of me, whether he approved of what I did, how proud he was (or wasn't)—it all mattered to me . . . a lot. I wanted him to walk into our house and think, "Wow! My girl's on it! Look how well she runs her house and cares for her family." The way the kids behaved, what they ate, how Rashawn and I interacted—everything felt under inspection, and I really wanted to pass the test.

It would be easy for me to say that I wanted a Pinterest-perfect house and a model family for my dad, but as I look back, it's clear that I actually wanted it for *me*. I wanted my dad's approval. I've always wanted it. If he was proud of me, then I'd feel enough—or so I thought. But as my desire for his applause grew louder in the days before his visit, I realized how impossible it would be to keep everything perfect (even for a few minutes). Let's get real: I've got two babies under two! What on earth was I thinking, trying to arrange the perfect grandparent visit?

Once I saw past my to-do list and into my heart, Jesus reminded me that his approval is what matters most. How kind of him to speak so lovingly and gently. He is so good!

God didn't want me to work for my dad's approval, but to serve from a place of approval—the eternal approval that Jesus died to give me. Serving from the reality that I'm already approved changes everything. True, I may still want to clean out the car; but having nothing to prove means that a trail of stray Cheerios or a spilled-milk stain won't feel like a withdrawal from the bank of my heart. When I trust that God approves of me, I can love and serve everyone—including my dad—without seeking their applause.

How are you doing with this, my friend? Has the approval or admiration of others ever influenced your choices? How we work or parent, where we buy our clothes, how much we serve at church, when we clean our house . . . if we're making these decisions mostly to impress others or to avoid their criticism, we're in trouble. If, like me, you've ever felt tempted to play for the crowd, if you've ever worried that others won't think you're good enough, knowing what God says about this issue will make a major difference.

Fear of What?

Some time ago a cartoon circulated the internet that shows two people looking at a headstone, apparently mourning someone they had lost. The tomb's inscription reads, "I apologize if my death saddens or inconveniences you." One of the cartoon figures remarks, "They say she was a chronic people pleaser."[1] Yikes!

Like with many cartoons, that's an exaggeration, but I think there's a lot of truth in it as well. This woman's identity literally got lost in an endless cycle of people-pleasing, and—even in death—what she cared about most was how others felt about her. What a prison!

The Bible has a name for this: the fear of man.

In case you're not familiar with that phrase, let's define what it means. It might help to start with what it doesn't mean. The fear of man does not mean that you're afraid of people, running in terror when there's no threat. Instead, the fear of man involves being more concerned with what others think of you than anything else. Fear of man means that you seek the approval of others so much that you're willing to sacrifice to secure their affirmation and acceptance.

Fear of man is a struggle nearly every person faces at some point. Most of us battle it a lot. Our need for acceptance, our desire for recognition and honor, pressure from people around us, our fear of criticism and humiliation . . . they all lead to the fear of man. And once we've been ensnared by the fear of man, we start to second-guess our decisions, doubt ourselves, and judge ourselves based on the opinions of others. If we fear man, we may lack boldness in our faith; we may even disobey God in an effort to please others.

Jasmyne, one of my beloved girlfriends, discovered this at her workplace. I'll let her share her story with you:

> I was the girl who actively avoided conflict with coworkers. I picked up extra tasks and said yes to win approval, even at the expense of my own peace. When colleagues got together to gossip or complain about work, I found myself laughing awkwardly and just going with the flow, even though a sour feeling in my stomach reminded me that, not only was I not being myself, I also wasn't honoring God. I was acting out of fear that my coworkers would reject me because I was a Christian and didn't do or say things like they did.
>
> This situation finally came to a head when invitations went out for an after-hours party celebrating a coworker moving on to another job. Even former colleagues were invited. Guess who wasn't? The person trying to please everyone. Yep. That was me.

I realized that, even if I wasn't doing everything my co-workers were doing, they could still tell I was different. And that was supposed to be a good thing! I had been sent by God to be a light in the darkness, not to blend into it. Though being excluded felt like a rude awakening for me at first, I quickly realized it was actually God lovingly calling me back to his purpose for me. I want to be the girl God made me to be, no matter what it costs. Sometimes being a friend of God means being rejected by others. I'm willing to take that risk. He's worth it.[2]

My dear friend learned in a painful way what Proverbs 29:25 teaches: "The fear of man lays a snare, but whoever trusts in the LORD is safe" (ESV). The peace God gives keeps us secure; our confidence comes from him. The fear of man is a trap that keeps us in chains.

Proverbs 29:25 reveals that the fear of man "lays a snare." I'm guessing that most of us don't regularly set traps to catch animals or birds, but we do know that snares are dangerous. You don't mess around with a bear trap. And if we were to ever get caught in a snare, we'd do whatever it took to break free.

Fear of man is the most dangerous of traps. No matter what we do, someone will be upset with us; pleasing others always requires more than we can give. The fear of man keeps us silent and intimidated; it fuels anxiety that we'll lose something we really want. But ultimately the fear of man is so dangerous because it displaces our identity as a set-apart, beloved daughter. It causes us to seek the approval of others more than we seek God. And that, my friend, is the definition of idolatry. Let me explain . . .

Free Indeed

When I read Luke 10:38–42, I imagine Martha caught up in needing to impress people with her hosting skills. I can so relate! Mary, on the other hand, dared to ignore the displeasure of others—*Help us clean! Help us cook!* Instead, she positioned herself as close to Jesus as possible. Mary chose worshiping Christ instead of worrying what others thought.

Just as the Bible calls people-pleasing the fear of man, it also has a phrase that describes the opposite: *the fear of the Lord.* The fear of the Lord is the antidote to the poison of people-pleasing. It's the power that sets us free from the trap of approval-seeking. While the fear of man makes us timid, fearful, and insecure, the fear of the Lord empowers us with boldness, peace, and confidence.

The fear of man is idolatrous because it puts others on the throne of our hearts; we want to please them more than we want to please God. The fear of the Lord, however, acknowledges Jesus's rightful place as the King of our lives, the Master of our destinies, the Alpha and Omega, the Beginning and the End.

When you see the phrase "the fear of the Lord," that doesn't mean being scared of God. That's not what his Word teaches. He is our beloved Father and does not want his set-apart daughters to cower before him.

When we truly know who God is, however, we tremble in awe of his majesty and holiness, his power and glory. The fear of the Lord cultivates a sacred awe and reverence for God in our hearts, a deep respect that motivates us to seek righteousness, act with faithfulness, and resist temptation. Having a healthy fear of God keeps us from living a life of sin. Proverbs 16:6 says simply and powerfully that "through the fear of the LORD evil is avoided."

God's holy presence exposes our sin, causing us to cry out in repentance. We see examples of this in the book of Isaiah, when the prophet relays God's words to Israel: "These are the ones I look on with favor: those who are humble and contrite in spirit, and who tremble at my word" (66:2). The apostle Paul fell to the ground when he encountered Jesus on the road to Damascus (Acts 9), and the apostle John was so overcome by the revelation of God's glory and the experience of his fullness that he "fell at his feet as though dead" (Rev. 1:17). The Lord responded to John in such a tender and beautiful way: "Then he placed his right hand on me and said: 'Do not be afraid. I am the First and the Last. I am the Living One; I was dead, and now look, I am alive for ever and ever!'" (Rev. 1:17–18).

Clearly, we are commanded not to be afraid. We are, however, called to worship God in the same kind of holy fear as Isaiah, Paul, John, and God's church across the ages experienced. To be in awe of him, to give him our complete devotion, to reject sin for his sake and for the purpose of revival, to honor him as the God of great glory, majesty, purity, and power—this is what the fear of the Lord means.

The Bible also tells us, "The fear of the LORD is the beginning of wisdom, and knowledge of the Holy One is understanding" (Prov. 9:10). In other words, if we want to be free of people-pleasing and start making wise decisions that honor Jesus, we need to develop a sacred reverence focused on pleasing God more than anyone else. This helps us abstain from sin, which is a huge part of living in freedom.

Fearing the Lord also protects us from the hurtful criticism and disapproval of others. When we're safely tucked in our heavenly Father's loving arms, we don't have to look to others for acceptance or security.

Doesn't that sound so reassuring? Isn't that what all of us really want—to be free from the lies that we've got to hold it all together, keep up appearances, and make everyone happy?

The reality is, if we leave the plans and purposes of our lives in the hands of others, we'll never become who God wants us to be. If we conform to what others want to see, we won't be free . . . ever. We'll live as slaves instead of as lavishly loved children. We'll be running around like Martha, seeking to impress rather than courageously and peacefully sitting at the feet of Jesus.

Jesus had the power to free Martha from people-pleasing in an instant. He could have whisked her concerns away without asking her to do anything at all. But Jesus did something better: he taught Martha what to do with her fear. Instead of removing her fear of disapproval, he invited Martha to transfer her affection and intention to the right place. I think of the story in Luke 10 as a lesson in fearing the Lord, not man, and loving and choosing Jesus above everything else.

God calls us to the same process of transformation. Instead of zapping away our fear of disapproval, he exposes our toxic fears and invites us to transfer that energy to fearing him out of reverence, awe, and deep love. When we face the false fear of disappointing others and deliberately decide that pleasing God matters more, others' criticism and our fixation on their approval lose power and force.

This is how it happened for my husband, Rashawn, the man I'm absolutely crazy about. I can't wait for you to get to know him.

What Kind of Hero Do You Want to Be?

When you're in fourth grade, nine or ten years old, the world should be wide open to you. You can still enjoy recess and be cool; you don't have the stress of puberty and all the zits, relationship drama, and awkwardness that comes with it. For a kid in fourth grade, there should still be childlike wonder and fun. Kids that age should not hear that their future is limited or that they should give up before things get worse, but that's basically what my beloved husband heard.

A shortsighted and unkind fourth-grade teacher told Rashawn that he should never pick up a pen and write again. The fleshly part of me wishes I could hand-deliver a copy of his book, *Start Where You Are,* to that teacher. I'd write "Guess what? You were dead wrong!" on a neon Post-it note and stick it to the cover. I just ache for the hurting little boy who grew up to be my amazing groom.

That message and the pressure to please at home set Rashawn on a very particular path to prove to everyone that he could be great. Tension and competition with other guys grew inside my husband as he started playing football. A desire to surpass his father's accomplishments caused Rashawn to push harder and fiercer. Battling with others for position, title, and accolades, Rashawn describes his teens and early adulthood in the military as a chaotic and unhealthy season, a time when he—and all the men around him—constantly put themselves on the throne of their life.

Ironically, to stay on the throne of your own heart, you have to seek approval. To keep the illusion going, you need people to affirm that "You're the man!" and "You got this!" You need others to think you're mighty and worthy in order to quiet the voice inside telling you that it could all come crashing down at any minute.

When Rashawn headed to LA as a young adult, seeking fame and fortune as an actor, the comparison trap ensnared him further. Everyone in Hollywood wanted to be seen, heard, and commended; everyone wanted to one-up each other. For my beloved husband, failure felt imminent all the time. Living for the applause of others nearly took him under.

After a radical conversion experience, Rashawn was delivered from the pit of people-pleasing and proving himself. He began seeking the approval of God alone. It wasn't easy, but Rashawn knew that it was right and good. He claimed Colossians 3:17 as a guiding verse: "Whatever you do, whether in word or deed, do it all in the name of the Lord Jesus, giving thanks to God the Father through him." Rashawn decided that his life would be about glorifying the Lord, not himself.

My husband spent years trying to be a hero, the guy everyone admired, counted on, wanted to be, and even feared. What he learned is that a true hero lays down their life in humility. A true hero is diligent in honoring the Lord and walks in step with the Spirit. A true hero has a fruitful life because they are faithful in prayer. A true hero keeps appointments with God to keep disappointments from killing their joy and peace. A true hero serves according to the example of Jesus. In surrendering his fury to prove himself a hero, my husband became one.

Don't get me wrong; I know Rashawn isn't perfect. I live with him, remember? But I see Jesus in Rashawn. I hear Jesus in his voice. I watch my husband serve with all his might, doing his best "to present [himself] to God as one approved, a worker who does not need to be ashamed and who correctly handles the word of truth" (2 Tim. 2:15). Rashawn no longer fights for acceptance and approval; he lives from it.

My sweetheart wants every woman reading this book to know that men also fight the desire for approval. The temptation may look different for our brothers in Christ, but we're all in this battle together. We need to encourage one another to reject the lies that we have to prove ourselves, that we're only as worthy as others think we are, that what we do defines who we are. Instead, I love what Rashawn had to say when I asked him about people-pleasing: "Instead of seeking their applause, praise and encourage others; give and don't reach. Be teachable and reachable, to God and to those in the body of Christ. What good is our ability if we're not available to God and others in love? Love God, love people, and you won't have to fixate on what others think about you."

It's Complicated

Like me, you probably wish that you could just decide to never again care about what people think. Since that's not realistic, we have to keep going back to God's truth. I love to meditate on Psalm 56:11 when I'm feeling overly concerned about people's opinions: "In God I have put my trust; I will not be afraid. What can man do to me?" (NKJV). So simple. So powerful.

Here's what's *not* simple, though: evaluating my own heart. When it comes to seeking the approval of others, I find that my heart often deceives me. I hate to think that I've sometimes served at church or even wanted others to see me as a woman who sits at the feet of Jesus in order to impress people, not to please God.

I remember one particular time when the Holy Spirit convicted me of this. Rashawn and I had been invited to serve at an Oklahoma City rescue mission. We arrived at the facility and began serving dinner to those who had no home, who struggled with addiction, who needed the warmth of food and affection they didn't receive anywhere else. Though there were several of us serving, I was the only mama, and I had our two babies along with us.

I'm sad to admit that I went into overdrive, wanting to impress everyone and show them that I could serve God and love people all while caring for two little ones. I wanted people to notice how well I could do both—that my boys could be well-behaved and I could minister to others at the same time.

When I got home and Jesus gently uncovered these motives of my heart, I felt so sad. How messy things get when I choose to do good, even godly, activities but my motivation is to impress others. Have you ever been tempted to pray in a certain way, say or do something at church, maybe even lead a study or worship service with the thought, "If people see that I'm super spiritual, then I'll feel accepted"?

I wonder if Martha convinced herself that she was cooking and cleaning and everything else for Jesus, when in reality she was serving to get noticed. I can't blame her, because I've been there myself! When I look back on times we've opened our home and the pressure I felt to make sure the house looked up-to-date, the desserts were the best anyone had ever eaten, and my fast-paced multitasking skills were on full display, I really empathize with Martha. Wanting to impress others—even Jesus—I can totally relate to that.

What I've learned and am still learning is that Jesus already approves of me. Psalm 147:11 declares, "The LORD takes pleasure in those who fear him, in those who hope in his steadfast love" (ESV). Every day I want to place my hope in God's love. I want my heart to be defined by the fear of the Lord, not the fear of man.

Don't forget, the person to whom we give the most authority in our lives—the one we let define our worth, direct what we do and how we do it, the one we look to most for approval—that's the person we fear most. The person we most want to impress, the one whose disapproval we're desperate to avoid, is also the person we will ultimately obey. That's why the fear of man is an idol and the fear of God is safe. He really, truly is God! Loving God and fearing him aren't opposites; they're like two sides of the same coin, inseparable and perfectly balanced.[3]

If you want to love God and serve him with reverent awe and respect, try giving something valuable to someone else, no strings attached. Consider taking what little spare time you have and offering to help the single mom down the street with yardwork. Spend time with the elderly, the homeless, the lost . . . without making sure that all of social media knows about your good deed. "Whatever you do," my friend, "work at it with all your heart, as working for the Lord, not for human masters" (Col. 3:23). Don't be mastered by others or seek their applause. Work for the Lord.

Before we close this chapter, I want to remind you that seeking the approval of God alone may mean doing things that make us uncomfortable. It may mean doing things that make others feel frustrated or confused. Sitting at the feet of Jesus didn't make Mary very popular, remember? But amazing things happen when we choose what is better. And as Jesus promised Mary, it will not be taken away from us (Luke 10:42).

I learned this in a powerful way when a coworker at the café where I worked in Oklahoma City began to experience symptoms of a heart attack. We immediately called 911 and helped our colleague to lie down. Waiting for the ambulance to arrive, the entire staff—including the top managers—gathered around. Just moments before, I had been busy with an important task that was really time-consuming. That didn't matter anymore; I felt profoundly moved by the Spirit to share the hope of Jesus with this man who was facing his own mortality.

I was also young and afraid of what people would think of me. The voice inside me whispered, *You can't leave your work and just pray for someone like that. Everyone will feel so awkward.* But I didn't want to obey that voice. I wanted to obey the Spirit. So I did.

Kneeling beside my coworker, I asked if I could pray for him. He nodded yes. I began to pray, then started to share about the hope found in Christ alone. God the Holy Spirit moved so powerfully. I sat at the feet of Jesus while I ministered to that person.

That day I chose the fear of the Lord over the fear of man. I don't always do this perfectly, but when I remember that experience, I know that I want to keep feeling the closeness with Jesus I enjoyed that day, not the stress I experience when I'm trying to impress others.

As I pray a blessing over us, consider what kind of life you want to live. I'm praying you'll live from God's approval, not for it.

Heavenly Father, *please help us to break our habit of seeking approval from anyone but you. Remind us through your Word that your Son, Jesus, paid the price for our sins, and because of that, we are approved by you for everlasting life. Thank you for accepting us as your beloved daughters and giving us a new identity in you. I pray that from now on we will seek to please you, Father, and not man. In Jesus's name, amen.*

6

SET APART
FROM WORRY

I DON'T KNOW what it's like for other women, but for me, becoming a mama opened floodgates of love . . . and anxiety.

If someone had told me how much I would adore my children, I would have believed them. But I was completely unprepared for how anxious I would feel about every detail of their little lives. *Are they hungry? Are they bored? Am I praying for them enough? Am I smart enough, positive enough, wise enough, godly enough to raise these little disciples?*

The worry felt like a never-ending cycle. I'd put my trust in Jesus for one thing, and almost instantly another worry would rise up to take its place. And then there were the times I realized I would make mistakes as a mom—I couldn't avoid that. It terrified me to think how much damage I could do by not knowing how to parent.

When Aiden was about eighteen months old, he developed a wheezing cough. I watched my firstborn labor to take shuddering breaths, and it nearly broke my heart. His fever soared, and I had no idea what to do. I had no clue how to tell if this was a life-threatening situation or not.

So, I turned to the place I trusted most: Google.

Of course, I don't *actually* trust Google more than anything. I'm a follower of Jesus for goodness' sake! But in those anxious moments when I felt so confused and helpless watching little Aiden suffer, I let fear drive me to the internet quicker than anywhere else.

Search engines can be helpful for many things. When you dive too deeply into medical issues, however, I find Google to be less than helpful. I wonder if there's been a study done about how many people end up at the emergency room thanks to internet medical diagnoses. I know I'm not the only one who's rushed to the ER after being online for too long!

The woman who sat at the admitting desk asked me a few easy questions . . . name, birthdate, symptoms. She looked up from her computer when I told her Aiden's temperature.

"Well, did you give him any Tylenol?" she barked.

In all fairness, maybe she didn't actually bark. But that's how it sounded to me. I was already feeling helpless. I was already doubting myself. I already felt like I wasn't a good enough mom to take care of my sick baby. Her question felt super aggressive and condemnatory. I explained that I didn't have any Tylenol at home and that I didn't know how much to give him.

Without taking a breath, this woman proceeded to tear me up one side and down the other. "How could you not give him Tylenol?" she accused, turning red in her frustration. "Don't you know he could have a seizure?" She went on with her tirade, but my brain turned to mush. Though she didn't say it, I basically heard, "Excuse me, but are you a complete failure?"

Up to this point, I had been trying really hard to remain calm. I kept asking Jesus to help me trust him, even though terror welled up inside of me. I was so scared, my friend, and I didn't want to be scared. I felt like the weight of the world was on me, and this woman piled shame on top of my already heavy-laden shoulders.

I completely broke down—but by God's grace the story doesn't end there.

A much kinder nurse took Aiden back to an exam room, and an empathetic doctor diagnosed him with RSV, a concerning but very treatable respiratory virus. They promised to help my sweet son, and they did. I didn't know what to do, but these medical professionals did. I can't tell you how grateful I was to leave the ER knowing that Aiden would be okay.

I could have left the hospital that night grateful for Aiden but ripping myself to shreds as a mama. I genuinely hadn't known about keeping Tylenol on hand in case a fever gets too high. I could have let this experience fill me with more fear about all that I didn't know and the potential harm that could cause my children. That would have been the easy route.

God was so kind to lead me down a different path. He spoke to me and helped me see that I could learn—even in my failures, even in my fears. I could either worry more or worship him with trust and thanksgiving. He protected Aiden when I couldn't. I saw that I could grow as a mama through a situation like this, learning what to do and what not to do. I saw that when fear wants to take control of me, I have a choice in the matter.

In chapter 3 we looked at how working from a place of prayer can displace worry in our lives. In this chapter I'd like to unpack how learning from our anxieties rather than leaning into them can transform our relationship with God, enabling us to own our giftedness in him and rest in who he's made us to be.

For many women, anxiety is a dizziness that disorients us and keeps us from experiencing the Prince of Peace. Battling anxiety may feel like a never-ending cycle to you. Even if you don't fight persistent worry, you may know others who do. Regardless of where you fall on the anxiety spectrum, learning more always helps. You ready for that?

Not My Circus . . . or Is It?

It strikes me that in Luke 10, Martha was working from an anxious posture. If she'd been at peace, I don't believe she would have complained to Jesus about her sister. Martha's heart may have been telling her to sit, to be with her friend Jesus, to rest rather than wrestle. Seems to me that she allowed anxiety over the meal, the house, and the event to win out. As with other dimensions of this story, I can absolutely relate to this.

I can also relate to Mary's desire to be quiet and at rest. I so want that! If Mary felt anxious about anything that evening, she sure didn't turn to Google for answers. No, she chose to be right where she needed to be—at the feet of the Prince of Peace. Remember that Jesus didn't praise Mary for being the perfect example of *everything*; instead, he acknowledged that being near to him mattered more than anything else. Whatever anxieties Mary had faced that day, she quieted them—for a time, at least—so that she could focus on the only One who mattered.

When I use my God-given gifts to serve my family and others but do so from a place of anxiety, it feels like the weight of the world hangs on my shoulders. Maybe, like me, you've sometimes felt trapped by fear. I can think of times when I've felt physically sick because of anxiety. Have you ever felt like you can't catch your breath? Or that your temper is so hot and short you might *actually* bite someone's head off? Or that the tightness in your chest might lead to a heart attack? If so, you're not alone!

And while physical symptoms heat up, anxiety also causes a raging inferno of thoughts. How is it that hundreds of thoughts can zoom through my mind at lightning speed when I'm anxious, but my brain is slow as molasses when I try to memorize Scripture? When I'm working or serving from an anxious heart, I start thinking about one thing that needs to be done, and next thing I know, an avalanche of *everything* that needs to be done from now until the day I die comes crashing down on me. Before I've even started, the stress makes me feel so behind that I literally can't do anything at all. How I hate feeling mentally paralyzed!

Anxiety doesn't stop with my body and mind, though. It also preys on my spirit. I know what I *should* do when I'm feeling anxious, but there are too many situations I can recall when I chose to remain worried because I believed I was in too deep to stop. What a lie! In those moments, I gave in to my weak and helpless feelings rather than embracing the sound mind that God has given me (see 2 Tim. 1:7). I surrendered to the suffocating attack of the enemy rather than arming myself with God's strength as I'm commanded to do in Ephesians 6:10–18.

Thankfully, there are also times when I surrender to the kindness and guidance of the Holy Spirit, when I respond to his gentle nudges to close my eyes, take deep breaths, and sit in silence with him. I may start playing a worship song or listen to the Word of God read out loud. I may rest in silence. But whatever the method, when I allow Jesus to quiet my heart, *everything* in me changes. My physical body resets, my mental energy gets channeled in healthy ways, and my spirit finds peace.

What has your experience with anxiety been like?

The women I minister to tell me that they feel anxious about their health or the health of family members, and COVID-19 has only increased these fears. As women, we worry about jobs and finding purpose. Relationships are also a huge source of stress and anxiety. Politics, racial tension, and the state of the world concern so many of us. Bills and financial worries top the list for many of my friends and colleagues.

As women, we can be anxious about everything from what to cook for dinner to whether we're meeting our family's spiritual needs. In both big and small things, we have a choice to make. We can't control our circumstances, but we can control where we allow our thoughts to go.

If I let my phone or my social media feed direct my thoughts, I'll never be free of anxiety. In this age of ringxiety, the most difficult battle for me is living in God's peace. Has this ever been true for you?

On days when I'm online more than I'm in the Word, things mostly fall apart. But when I choose to spend time in the secret place with my heavenly Father, he puts the pieces of my life back together. In 2 Corinthians 1:3–4, Paul describes the Lord as the "Father of compassion and the God of all comfort, who comforts us in all our troubles." Isn't that just beautiful? I want to be at peace with him more than anything. But sometimes it's hard to know how to do that in practical terms, isn't it? So let's look at some specific things we can do to step away from anxiety and keep in step with the Spirit instead.

Peace or Panic . . . You Choose

Anxiety follows two relatively predictable paths in our minds. The first is "What if . . . ?" *What if that lump is cancer? What if my husband is the next one to be laid off? What if there's another pandemic? What if things never change?* The "what ifs" of life can paralyze us with fear of the future.

The second path our minds travel when we feel anxious is "If only . . ." *If only I hadn't made that foolish choice as a teenager. If only I had eaten better or worked out more. If only I had followed all the advice I got when my kids were little.* "If only" traps us in regret, guilt, and shame over our past.

Have you ever faced "what if?" or "if only" battles in your mind?

Like many women, I deal with these a lot. Some days I'm consumed by anxiety. Other days I experience the Holy Spirit's victory—I love those days! And I've come to see some specific patterns and ways that help me have more overcoming days and fewer overwhelmed days.

The Word of God is the anchor that keeps me from drifting down the paths of "what if?" (fear of the future) and "if only" (anxiety about the past). With the prophet Jeremiah, "This I call to mind and therefore I have hope: Because of the LORD's great love we are not consumed, for his compassions never fail. They are new every morning; great is your faithfulness" (Lam. 3:21–23).

There is not one morning that I don't wake up to God's mercy. Help is available for me every single day. It's there for you too. Sister, we have hope because of that! Because of his great love, we don't have to be consumed by anxiety. God's compassion never fails! That is *good news*, my friend.

His truth strengthens me when I fear that I'm not enough for what I face. The apostle Peter reminds us that Jesus "has given us *everything* we need to live and to serve God" (2 Pet. 1:3 NCV). What I have is enough for this day, this moment, and every moment to come. God promises this, and he who promises *is* faithful (see Heb. 10:23 for a fantastic reminder of this truth).

As you can see, filling my mind with the Word of God is my number one strategy when facing anxiety. I remember reading a phrase by John Piper that really helped me with this: "Read the Bible to your anxiety."[1] Isn't that a great idea? Instead of listening to your anxiety, talk to it. And don't just repeat some I'm-gonna-get-you phrases of self-empowerment. Fight your worry with fire—the consuming fire of God's truth!

In the battle against anxiety, I take 2 Corinthians 10:4–5 very seriously: "The weapons we fight with are not the weapons of the world. On the contrary, they have divine power to demolish strongholds. We demolish arguments and every pretension that sets itself up against the knowledge of God, and we take captive every thought to make it obedient to Christ." I can't control my circumstances, but I can control which path I allow my thoughts to travel down. I can be captivated by anxiety, or I can take anxiety captive.

When worry turns into fear and fear turns into anxiety and anxiety tries to suffocate me, I deliberately choose to turn my thoughts back to Jesus. Sometimes this feels like a war inside my own head, but I know that I need to stop myself from getting on the anxiety train. Even if it feels like the hardest thing in the world to do—because, friend, we all know how easy it is to give in to anxiety—I ask God to shift my focus back to him. I ask him to fill me with his peace, knowing he is at work even when I can't understand what he's up to. I ask him to remind me of and help me hold on to the promise that he knows exactly what I need. As peace starts to transform my thinking, I ask for contentment and the ability to see that he has something for me right where I'm at—good works prepared in advance for me to walk in (Eph. 2:10). We can't operate from our giftedness if we're surrendering to anxiety.

Depending on how intense a situation is, the whole process of taking our thoughts captive may last a few moments, or it may last several days. However long it takes, the key to experiencing peace rather than panic is staying in step with God the Holy Spirit.

Once upon a time, I learned this in a really cool way . . .

When Rashawn and I first got married, we were totally broke. We still hosted people in our home, though, and one night a friend brought his buddy Dean over for Bible study. Dean had a videography business, and when it came time to share prayer requests, he shared that his business was really struggling. Through the course of the evening, both Rashawn and I felt the Holy Spirit leading us to give Dean three hundred dollars. Sister, that was three hundred dollars we desperately needed ourselves!

Anxiety tried to creep in at the thought of being what seemed almost recklessly generous, but I knew the Spirit was working. We felt God equipping us for the work of generosity, so Rashawn and I obeyed the Spirit's call. Before Dean left, we gave him the money. He was completely blown away. And I'm not exaggerating when I tell you that gift ended up turning his business around and changing his life!

A few days later, our friend Elise handed us three hundred dollars and said God had told her to give it to us. I couldn't have written a more powerful script!

If I had listened to the anxiety welling up inside me, Dean wouldn't have received what he needed that day. If Elise had listened to an internal voice telling her to forget about it, to move on, to ignore God's prompting, then we wouldn't have been blessed and helped either. When we allow the Spirit to take our anxiety captive, when we surrender to his plans and purposes and walk in step with him, our fear has to submit to the Prince of Peace.

In Luke 10 Jesus invited Martha to experience that peace by choosing what is better. From Jesus's teachings on worry in his Sermon on the Mount (see Matt. 6), we know that fighting anxiety is not about being strong enough to vanquish every fear; that would be impossible. Instead, it's about listening more to the voice of God the Holy Spirit and less to the voice of our anxiety. We can tune out the concerns and details that don't matter and trust the Spirit to guide us in doing something about the fears we need to face.

The closer we are to God, the more we can hear the Spirit's voice. On the other hand, "Our anxiety often shows us that we are too close to the world and too far from God."[2]

You probably want to get closer to God and farther from anxiety as much as I do, so how can we learn to better listen for the words of peace and truth we need? Let's turn our attention to that now.

Taking Worry into Worship

Unfortunately for me and Rashawn, Aiden's RSV isn't the only thing that's taken us to the ER. When we were young marrieds, we actually ended up at the hospital a few other times thanks to our frenemy Google. Overwhelmed with anxiety, I'd type out our symptoms and quickly determine one of us was going to die. Late-night trips to discover that you're perfectly healthy—despite what the internet claims—only lead to mounting medical bills and a whole bunch of regret. I know some of you out there can relate!

I bring this up because health issues have been a major source of worry for me. Health concerns have also become a place in which God the Holy Spirit has invited me to deeper communion with him. By the time the COVID-19 pandemic hit, I could see how much God had worked in me, teaching me to take my worries into worship.

Remember, I did not grow up being discipled in a close personal relationship with God. I knew about religion, but I had no clue how to walk in step with the Spirit or listen for his voice. As I began to spend time with God, meeting him in the secret place where it was just me and him with his Word open before me, I started to experience something I never imagined was possible. I began to hear his voice.

It would come to me through a Scripture I read or a worship song that played in the background of my mind. As I invited God into every aspect of my day, asking him to guide where I went, who I talked to, what to say (or not to say!), and when to stop and be quiet with him, I truly heard the Spirit's voice. He directed me to use my gifts for him every day. I once thought that was only for super-Christians, but the Holy Spirit wanted to be in constant communion with me. How awesome is that?

He longs to show you that love and be that close to you too, my friend. I've found that we can hear the Spirit best when we choose to be quiet and still at some point during our day. As a mama of two boys under age two, I know how hard having extended quiet times can be. Even if it's only a few moments of stillness while little ones are sleeping or on your ten-minute break at work, God can and will meet you right where you are. If you have an extremely consuming job, maybe turning off the radio during your drive to work can give you a couple quiet moments to hear from the Lord. Whatever it takes, choose to quiet your soul for at least a few minutes each day.

Most of the time people talk at God. We tend to give him a list of all the things that are wrong. There's nothing wrong with asking God for help; he invites us to do that. But if we never silence our minds and our thoughts, we won't hear from God. I promise, choosing to quiet your mind for even a few moments every day will change you so, so much. Our anxieties won't last when we're in the presence of God the Holy Spirit.

I've also found that the more I feed my spirit with the Word of God, the clearer I can hear the Holy Spirit speak. The Spirit's voice is like the fresh air of peace that transforms the suffocating atmosphere of anxiety.

Two of my favorite verses for fighting anxiety are John 14:27 and Philippians 4:6–7. I encourage you to write out these verses, stick them on your mirror or in your kitchen, and meditate on them every single day. As you do, you'll be better able to hear God's voice the next time you're feeling anxious.

Jesus promises, "Peace I leave with you; my peace I give you. I do not give to you as the world gives. Do not let your hearts be troubled and do not be afraid" (John 14:27).

You are not alone in your anxiety. God doesn't give us a worldly "peace of mind" that lasts only as long as things are going well. Instead, he gives us peace that lasts. He also gives us a great weapon in fighting anxiety.

Philippians 4:6–7 commands, "Do not be anxious about anything, but in every situation, by prayer and petition, with thanksgiving, present your requests to God. And the peace of God, which transcends all understanding, will guard your hearts and your minds in Christ Jesus." Gratitude is the weapon God gives us in fighting anxiety. He actually designed our brains in such a way that it's impossible to give thanks and be anxious at the same moment.

If you're eager to walk in step with the Spirit, take your worry into your worship. You don't have to get rid of anxiety before you can thank God for who he is and for all he's done. Take your worry right into the throne room and cast it at the feet of Jesus, just like 1 Peter 5:7 tells us to do. He cares about you! He cares about me! And as we choose to worship, we can hear the Spirit speak over our anxious thoughts. His voice then becomes louder than our fears.

When the clouds of anxiety start spreading shadows over God's promises, take those worries into your worship. The

Spirit is strong enough to break through the clouds. If your anxieties are rolling over you like a tide, take that worry into the sanctuary. You can't think your way out of everything, but you can worship your way through it.

Dear one, I know this isn't easy. But living with crushing anxiety isn't easy either, is it?

As we close this chapter, I want to share a post written by my beloved husband that helped me so much during the COVID-19 outbreak. As Rashawn's words remind you that the world cannot take away the peace Jesus died to give us, that no pandemic or lack of resources can negate God's presence and provision, I pray you'll be as encouraged as I was.

> The word *peace* in the world means to be without problems, conflict, or stress. However, the peace that Jesus offers is something that the world cannot give or take away.
>
> - The peace Jesus offers defies circumstances.
> - The peace Jesus offers defies logic.
>
> I can remember thinking, How is that even possible? . . . How can we have peace amidst a world full of chaos? . . . For someone who has never experienced it, that kind of peace can seem unattainable or impossible . . . but Jesus is the Prince of Peace. He can speak one word and calm the winds and waves—and He can do the same thing with your heart full of fear, anxiety, and depression. . . .
>
> The apostle Peter stepped out of the boat right during the middle of a treacherous storm [see Matt. 14:22–33]. . . . As long as he focused on Jesus, he was at peace and oblivious to the stormy waves that were crashing around him. As soon as he took his eyes off of the Lord and focused on what was

going on around him, he became fearful and he ended up getting swallowed up by the waves.

Beloved, our circumstances may not change, but our attitude can, and that is enough to find His peace. Peter had to lose his fear and take a giant leap of faith to step out of that boat, and Christ calls us to take a step of faith as well.

Listen! Honestly, the world cannot give us Christ's peace, and it can't take it away from us. . . .

May you find the confidence in God's presence today to step out in courage, to let go of all the futile things which hold you back and step out in God's power to joyfully receive the peace that Jesus is offering you today.[3]

Pray with me, dear one, that we might receive that peace . . .

Father, *King of Glory, we thank you for being sovereign over our lives and over our circumstances. Thank you, Jesus, for being the Prince of Peace. Father, we confess there have been many times when we have allowed anxiety to sweep over us instead of allowing your peace to reign in our hearts and minds. I pray, Lord, that you will help us to trust you, to surrender to you all our cares and worries. Help us to live our lives fully surrendered to and dependent on you. In Jesus's name, amen.*

7

SET APART
IN REST

Rest.

What comes to mind when you read that word?

Do you regularly rest? Do you even know how?

For a long time, I would have answered no to those last two questions.

Growing up in Puerto Rico, I rarely saw any lazy people. Puerto Ricans just can't stand laziness. It's work, work, work all day, sleep in exhaustion at night, and get up to do it again, day after day after day. Productivity is praised; the smallest hint of laziness brings criticism and condemnation. One of the things Puerto Rican parents fear most is raising children without a strong work ethic.

Every Saturday morning around seven o'clock, I awoke to my mom's radio blasting salsa or bachata music. From our earliest childhood days, my sister and I associated the radio with one thing: chores. It was like a drill, Saturday after Saturday. Mom didn't even have to wake us up; she let blaring Latin American rhythms do that for her.

My friend, I did not take kindly to this as I got older. I remember waking up so many weekends in total aggravation. It didn't matter that I had been up early every other day that week to get to school. It didn't matter that I wanted to sleep in . . . just once. There were floors to be mopped, meals to be cooked, laundry to be washed and hung (no electric dryers for us). In PR, people even clean their driveways.

Because most houses in Puerto Rico have no air-conditioning and the weather goes from hot to scorching, sleeping with a standing fan—usually pointed directly at my face—was an absolute necessity. Trouble is, when you live almost every moment with the windows open in your apartment, a whole lot of dust collects in the slats of each precious fan. Cleaning those beasts and taking the screens out of my windows to wash and spray with water (another way Puerto Ricans beat the heat) was not my idea of a chillaxed Saturday. But, again, my opinion in this didn't matter.

Mom continually told my sister and me, "The earlier you learn to do these things well, the better. No man wants to marry a lazy, disorganized woman. And even if you don't get married, you need to know how to do these things so that you won't have to rely on anyone else." Independence and competence were much more important to my mom than rest.

It certainly wasn't just my family that approached life this way. Everywhere I went, someone was cleaning or cooking, and I was expected to jump in. In PR, if you're not busy, something's wrong. Both my grandmas loved to clean. Like, *loved* to clean. I never saw Puerto Rican women stop— except maybe the very old or the very sick. If you weren't busy with your own work, you were outside helping and socializing with your neighbors.

When I got to the US, I was completely shocked to find out you could live near people and never know them. Puerto Ricans don't hide in their houses and mind their own business. Everything is considered *everyone's* business. You're constantly hosting your neighbors, borrowing something from them or lending something to them, and helping with this, that, and whatever. What I'm trying to say is that I never saw an example of rest when I was growing up.

And yet, there were moments when I longed to just listen to the birds sing or watch the trees sway outside my window. I wish you could see the amazing groves of plantain trees stretching as far as the eye can see on my island home. Or that you could smell the *sofrito* and *sazón* spices simmering on the stove as they're stirred into rice at just the right moment. Sometimes I wanted to get lost in that scent or in the bursting flavors and dynamic colors of the traditional dishes my grandma taught me to cook. I realize now that I ached to stop and savor, to just live in the moment, but that wasn't something we did in PR. Sure, people may have noticed and even appreciated such things, but then they were on to the next thing at lightning speed. There was no stopping.

Over time, this perpetual busyness led me to believe that the minute I wasn't doing anything, I was in trouble. I felt guilty if I wasn't busy or helping someone who was. If my sister and I didn't know what to do, Mom would gladly—and quickly!—figure it out for us. I never asked why we lived this way; I never even wondered if it was good or right. That's just how things were.

Fast-forward to the days just before Jesus set me free. I was a young woman in the US living just like I did in PR—at a furious, never-stopping pace. I worked hard, played hard, and rested never. Then God met me, and I began to learn his ways of living. I studied his commandments but had a hard time understanding Sabbath rest.

Though I had heard of the Ten Commandments as a child in church, I honestly forgot that resting made it on God's top-ten list. I remembered what I considered the "big" commandments—don't lie, don't steal, don't kill. But rest? That seemed like such a waste of time. Why would I do that? I didn't want to disobey God; I just couldn't wrap my head around it. This confusion persisted into the early days of my marriage.

Then I had babies.

I never imagined that I could crave quiet, calm, and sleep *so much.* Before Aiden and Eliyah were born, I might have tried to honor the Sabbath because that's what God said to do, but after the boys came, I yearned for rest. And not just physical rest. My soul ached to be at rest too.

I wanted rest but didn't know how to get it. I had trained myself to be so efficient, so busy, so productive, that I felt restless whenever I tried to rest.

You may or may not have grown up in a hyperbusy environment like I did, but I've been around enough women to know that true rest is difficult to come by, challenging to understand, and yet deeply craved by many of us. God made us to rest, so of course our bodies and souls cry out for it. Like everything else, though, we must learn how to do it.

You Who Are Weary

We genuinely don't know what emotions Mary carried into the house the night she and Martha hosted Jesus. We also have no idea what baggage weighed on Martha. Did they have an amazing day, or were they hurting? Had they been super busy all week? Were they excited or exhausted at the thought of entertaining? Kinda crazy to think about these dynamics, isn't it?

Again, focusing on only one aspect of the Luke 10 story limits our perspective. It's essential that we acknowledge, as Jesus himself declares in verse 42, that sitting at the feet of Jesus was the better choice. However, it's also important to recognize that it wasn't just Mary's physical posture of sitting quietly that Jesus praised. Mary's soul was at rest in that moment, while her sister's soul was distracted, worried, and upset (vv. 40–41).

For women in a nonstop world, this is huge. We can physically cease working but never allow our souls to rest. In other words, we can rest our bodies and still be restless inside.

Have you ever spent a whole day doing things that are supposed to be restful, only to feel tired and/or anxious when you lie down to sleep? Maybe you hit the salon for a mani-pedi, binge-watched several episodes on your favorite streaming platform, and window-shopped at the mall or online. Maybe you were even on vacation. You weren't working, but you didn't feel at peace afterward. You came home to the same concerns that you left with. In fact, you carried them with you into the nail salon or on your vacation. You may have bought pretty things or watched funny and romantic stories, but you didn't truly rest.

After one particularly difficult day, I remember telling Rashawn that I just needed some space. I asked him, "Can I please get away for a couple hours?" My sweet husband said, "No problem," so I got in my car and drove . . . somewhat aimlessly.

I ended up at Target, browsing up and down every aisle, looking at all the lovely décor in the home section, wondering what some of the fashionable clothes would look like on me (but having no energy to try them on), listening to the faint music pumping through the speakers and the endless hum of the newest electronic devices. It was calm, pretty quiet, and devoid of any work. But I got home and felt no better.

That night I saw—more clearly than I ever had before—that not all rest is created equal. I needed to learn not just to rest from my labor but to enter into the soul rest that Jesus died to give me.

In Matthew 11:28–30, Jesus extends an invitation: "Come to me, all you who are weary and burdened, and I will give you rest. Take my yoke upon you and learn from me, for I am gentle and humble in heart, and you will find rest for your souls. For my yoke is easy and my burden is light." Our loving Savior won't force us to rest, but he will give us rest if we come to him. That's why resting only through self-care strategies never ultimately satisfies.

Yes, we need to care for our physical bodies and to do that lovingly and well. Sister, I love a good mani-pedi as much as anyone. But if salon time, entertainment, shopping, or even vacations are the extent of our relaxation, we haven't entered true rest. We've substituted simply stopping for true soul care, and that's a damaging trade.

I think that's why Jesus includes the idea of learning in his invitation from Matthew 11. "Learn from me," he urges, "and you will find rest for your souls."

We can't go back in time and peer into Mary's and Martha's souls, but if we could, I suspect we'd see that sitting at the feet of Jesus is a reflection of what every woman—even Martha!—truly longs for: a soul at rest.

In Psalm 62:1, King David exclaims, "Truly my soul finds rest in God; my salvation comes from him." Other translations read, "In God alone my soul finds rest" (BSB) and "My soul rests quietly only when it looks to God" (ISV). Isn't that beautiful and so, so true?

The first step in learning from Jesus how to rest involves recognizing that we find rest *only* in him. If we're ever to genuinely rest, we must learn not simply to stop or even just to relax and be quiet or calm. We must also enter the soul rest only our Lord gives. Fortunately, God teaches and models this very thing for us.

Asleep at the Wheel . . . or on a Cushion

When I first met Rashawn, I could not believe how slowly he did everything. That may sound like an insult, but it's absolutely not. My husband is so patient. His attitude is always, "Don't rush," "Take your time," and "We have all the time in the world to get these things done."

Imagine how this clashed with my upbringing. And I didn't even mention my dad in my earlier description. He's a super fast-paced guy, always metaphorically (and sometimes literally) snapping his fingers in a "Let's get this down NOW!" kind of way. After I got to the US, everything went at a fast-forward, there's-no-time-to-waste pace.

Getting to know Rashawn, I was struck by the air of calm about him. He almost never expressed impatience. To this day he's always the last one to get in or out of the car. After we had the boys, I'd be out with both of them before he'd even open the driver's side door. I had no idea how that was possible!

But I watched Rashawn be in the moment, at peace, physically slow because he was spiritually calm. I admired that. I wanted it. I needed his example. Rashawn helped me see that slowing down doesn't equal being unproductive, that taking your time doesn't equal wasting it, that hurry doesn't equal efficiency. God knew exactly what he was doing in putting the two of us together!

Rashawn sets a Christlike example for me when it comes to learning to rest well and truly. Once upon a time, I'd internally scoff whenever my sweet husband would encourage me to take a nap. Now I see that taking a nap may be the holiest thing I do on a Sabbath day.

Resting may not confuse my husband, but it does confuse a lot of people. Even the twelve disciples felt perplexed and a bit aggravated by Jesus's example of rest, as we see in Mark's account of him calming the storm (4:36–40).

When he walked on earth, Jesus could have served and worked nonstop. There were as many needs in the first century as there are today—sick people, heartbroken people, angry and lost people. They crowded around Jesus almost every minute. One evening, though, Jesus and his disciples left the crowd behind, got in a boat, and set out for the other side of the lake. "There were also other boats with him. A furious squall came up, and the waves broke over the boat, so that it was nearly swamped. Jesus was in the stern, sleeping on a cushion. The disciples woke him and said to him, 'Teacher, don't you care if we drown?' He got up, rebuked the wind and said to the waves, 'Quiet! Be still!' Then the wind died down and it was completely calm" (Mark 4:36–39).

Can you imagine the disciples' shock? Jesus, the same man who brought sight to the blind and revealed the intention of every heart, was sleeping cluelessly (or so they thought) while a furious storm raged, threatening to sink the boat and cast everyone into the deep. They woke Jesus up (*not* by blaring Latin American bachata music, I'm guessing) and asked him a similar question to the one Martha asked in Luke 10: "Don't you care, Lord?"

In this moment, Jesus showed the disciples that we don't have to let our outward circumstances dictate whether our souls are at rest. He didn't allow the storm to disrupt his rest, which he needed both physically and emotionally. Jesus took on human form when he came to earth; that means he sometimes felt weary and heavy-laden just like we do. Jesus used this situation on the lake to teach his disciples that whether they were in stormy seas or outwardly at peace, their souls could find rest in him alone.

At Jesus's command the wind and waves stopped. Before that he had been resting in the stern, and I like to imagine that afterward he went right back to sleep on his cozy cushion. Though innumerable crowds needed him, though the storm had been raging around him, Jesus stopped to rest.

As we noted earlier, the first step in learning to rest well is recognizing that our souls find rest only in God. The story of Jesus sleeping through the storm reveals a second dynamic in learning soul rest: it can be found no matter what our circumstances are like.

If we wait for our chaotic world to stop spinning and our overfull lives to slow down, we will never rest. Jesus modeled resting in the storm so that we can learn from him and accept his invitation: "Come to me, all you who are weary and heavy-laden . . ."

I remember sitting in my car one day and feeling so tired. I didn't want to do anything. I just sat there in the stillness as worship music played lightly in the background. And God the Holy Spirit spoke to me: "Come, Denisse. I know you are weary and burdened." I felt his call, his kindness, his mercy.

Not long before this, I had come across something that touched on this theme—though my mommy brain can't remember precisely where I read it. The basic idea is that no one burns out by doing the right things. We burn out because of what we *don't* do. If I didn't rest, burnout would overtake me. God brought those words to mind as I reflected on his invitation to rest. In those quiet moments I embraced the truth that, in order to be who God made me to be, in order to do the Father's work well, I have to rest no matter what's happening in my house, my ministry, and my relationships. We can't allow circumstances to determine whether our souls are at rest.

We often focus on so many nonessentials that keep us from true rest. We can also work day and night on good things, even on kingdom things, and still burn out. Jesus invites us to learn that we can find rest *only* in him and that we can rest no matter what's going on in our lives. In order to do that, I believe we need to recapture a practice that God commanded long ago. We need to embrace the practice of Sabbath rest if we are to learn from Jesus and receive his rest.

A Whole Day?!

In Exodus 20:1–2 we're told, "God spoke all these words: 'I am the LORD your God, who brought you out of Egypt, out of the land of slavery. You shall have no other gods before me.'" The Lord gave Moses a list of commands that would guide the actions of his people, Israel. Today, even nonreligious people recognize the moral benefits of the Ten Commandments. Whether you're a Christian or not, it's clear that human life flourishes when people don't steal, lie, murder, or envy.

Right in the middle of the Ten Commandments we find this decree: "Remember the Sabbath day by keeping it holy. Six days you shall labor and do all your work, but the seventh day is a sabbath to the LORD your God. On it you shall not do any work. . . . For in six days the LORD made the heavens and the earth, the sea, and all that is in them, but he rested on the seventh day. Therefore the LORD blessed the Sabbath day and made it holy" (Exod. 20:8–11).

There are some interesting things to note about this commandment. For starters, eight of the other nine commandments are stated in far fewer words; God's command to practice the Sabbath, with its lengthy explanation, stands out as a major exception. I think that's important. God doesn't overuse words like a student who is trying to meet an essay requirement. His Word is always purposeful and carefully chosen. Perhaps God knew we'd need more details when it comes to the Sabbath.

I also find it fascinating that God starts this commandment with the word "remember." I really believe he knew we'd forget the Sabbath, that we'd need to be reminded. We need to remember that God Almighty, who created everything that's ever been or ever will be, rested from his work on the seventh day. If God rested, if he blessed the Sabbath day and made it holy, don't you think we should follow his example?

Perhaps one reason people don't practice true Sabbath rest is that they have false ideas about it. Maybe they think the Sabbath has to be observed on Sunday in order to count. But what about people who have to work on Sunday— including church staff? Does that mean they get no Sabbath? While God's people in ancient times rested on the same day of the week (Saturday), in modern times we can rest with grace. We may enjoy Sabbath rest on any day of the week.

A lot of people also have false ideas about what you may and may not do on the Sabbath. This hinders us from enjoying Sabbath rest. Remember, the Pharisees were the ones with the most rigid Sabbath rules and the ones Jesus spoke against most passionately. Sabbath rest isn't about following a bunch of dos and don'ts.

Like I once did, some people believe Sabbath rest is a waste of time. In our modern age, when productiveness is next to (or even more important than) godliness, resting for *a whole day* seems almost irresponsible. How will we get ahead if we don't keep up with people who are working all the time? How will we accomplish our goals and make it to retirement on time if we don't push now?

I understand these questions and concerns. Honestly, I think Martha would have understood them too. It seems like her thoughts traveled down the same kind of road. *How can I manage all of this? How will everything get done if Mary*

*just sits there? It's not fair that she gets to be with Jesus while I'm
stuck in here making all the food and arranging all the details.*

Perhaps such thoughts about Sabbath rest reveal what we
really believe. Maybe they show that we think in order to
truly live, we must do or have [fill in the blank]. If we're hoping to keep up with the latest house, toys, and electronics,
then working nonstop is nonnegotiable. If we measure our
worth by our work—even our service at home or church—
slowing down will produce guilt and shame. But what if it
doesn't have to be this way?

Jesus never equated work with worth. He has given us
spiritual gifts and desires us to use them with joy and diligence, but those gifts also come with boundaries (the Sabbath command) and an invitation. He urged the disciples,
"Come with me by yourselves to a quiet place and get some
rest" (Mark 6:31). What an offer! God is not a slave driver
who wants us to work, work, work until we die. The Lord
reminds us, "In vain you rise early and stay up late, toiling
for food to eat—for he [God] grants sleep to those he loves"
(Ps. 127:2).

Even though Sabbath rest is a commandment, not an
option, God still allows us to choose our path. We can rise
up early and stay up late, toiling from start to finish, but we
will never truly flourish. We'll find ourselves like Martha:
distracted, worried, and upset. Maybe God *commands* us to
remember the Sabbath because he knows how hard it is for
us to choose it ourselves.

Does resting for a whole day feel like a frightening pros-
pect or the most exhilarating invitation? You get to choose.
Week after week, I'm trying to choose wisely, to rest truly,
to find peace for my soul. What about you?

Apply, Don't Deny

God has given us rest. He's commanded us to rest. Yet still we may deny ourselves that gift of his grace. Instead of denying yourself, I pray that you'll apply the truths of this chapter to your life in practical ways.

When I first started learning to practice Sabbath rest, I really had no idea what to do. Was I supposed to sit on the couch all day reading Scripture and praying while my kids ran around like wild banshees? Somehow I didn't think God would see that as a good idea.

By the time I had both Aiden and Eliyah, I learned that not all rest is created equal, and I wanted true rest for my soul. I had discovered that I could find true rest in God alone, and he had taught me that I could have rest despite my circumstances. What remained was learning specific ways that my body, mind, and spirit were made to rest. Back then I was super grateful for two online teachers who helped me learn practical ways to enjoy Sabbath rest.

One woman helped me see the tremendous blessing of spending time in God's creation on the Sabbath. She often talked about and even posted videos of the time she spent enjoying her garden or sitting on her patio listening to the wind in the trees. She built fires in her fireplace and watched the flames. She sipped tea to refresh her body and talked with her loved ones to refresh her mind. Being a girl who also loves nature and the visual pictures God has placed in creation, I really resonated with these suggestions for Sabbath rest. I love taking leisurely walks in botanical gardens or through luscious parks. I adore the ocean and find such soul rest at the shore.

I know these things aren't for everyone, and that's okay. My encouragement is to find the things that are life-giving for *you*.

Another woman who helped me is a mother of three young children. She showed me that even in the often-stormy season of raising toddlers, true rest can be enjoyed. She talked about and modeled preparing meals and finishing chores ahead of time so she could be with her kids on the Sabbath, coloring with them or doing simple crafts with things they found in the house or backyard. Again, this might not be your idea of Sabbath rest, but it spoke to me. Having unhurried time with my boys for fun and creativity is a restful blessing for me.

Rashawn and I sometimes spend the Sabbath loving on the homeless community, taking food and gift cards, prayer and encouragement to the needy on Oklahoma City's streets. *That's restful?* you might wonder. For us it can be deeply renewing for our souls to follow the example of Jesus and be his hands and feet. Jesus healed people and served on the Sabbath. In his strength and peace, so can we. Sabbath rest does not automatically mean staying at home; blessing others can refresh us as well.

Beyond these ideas, which may be more enjoyable for some than for others, there are certain things that help all of us find true rest. Relishing rather than rushing time in God's Word, not just playing worship music but entering into worship, and allowing our souls to be quiet enough to hear from the Holy Spirit—these are gateways to soul rest for all God's set-apart daughters.

God also invites us to lay aside the expectations of others as a discipline of Sabbath rest. Chances are, the minute you try to rest, someone will want something from you. Even if they don't mean to load you down, other people can unwittingly compound your stress by adding to your schedule. Like a rubber band, though, the more you get stretched, the faster you'll break.

Sabbath rest involves saying no to stretched-to-the-breaking-point living. If we always say yes to people because we're afraid that we'll let them down, we sacrifice time with the Lord and ultimately may disobey his command to rest. Before anything goes on your Sabbath day calendar, ask the Lord for his direction. He will let you know if an activity is an invitation from him or an expectation from someone else.

Sister, denying yourself Sabbath rest is not only unhealthy—it's also unholy. Apply yourself to learning from Jesus and practicing what *The Message* calls "the unforced rhythms of grace" (see Matt. 11:28–30). You will find rest for your souls. Beloved one, doesn't that sound good?

> **Father**, *in Jesus's name I thank you that true rest, rest that this world cannot give, is found in you. I pray for the weary woman who needs rest but doesn't know how to get it. Father, I pray that you will pull her closer to your heart and remind her that, in you, there is rest for her soul. You are the giver of rest. I pray that she will come to you and that you will refresh her and renew her strength. We look forward to the day when we will experience true, eternal rest with you in glory.*
>
> *I bless each reader in the name of Jesus. Amen.*

8

SET APART
IN LOVE

IT'S EXTREMELY RARE for a week go by without a text or call
from my grandma, or a package from her arriving in the mail
for me, the boys, and Rashawn, or some other demonstration
of her love blessing our family. Though we've lived in different countries for many years now, my grandma's love has
never faltered, never changed, never stopped. Her generosity astounds me. She sends money to me and my sister.
She buys plane tickets for our family of four to visit her. I'm
telling you, my grandmother loves *lavishly*. It's her voice I
remember speaking the words "I love you" to me as a little
girl. I am so grateful for her!

Perhaps my grandma's love has been all the more special
and important to me because I can't remember hearing "I
love you" very often as a child.

It's possible, I suppose, that people around me did use
those words. Still, love felt foreign, and I believed it so little
that my memory comes up blank when thinking about positive emotions from my early years. What I do remember is

hearing, "I wish you were never born." I remember rage and cigarettes and booze and being hit. I wish I could forget, but I remember.

My life felt like an endless cycle of school, work, and chores. Grandma's love was a gift from God in the midst of my heartache. Without her care and concern, I'm not sure where I'd be. I truly believe my heavenly Father used my grandmother to set an example of genuine love, love that could last, love that sacrificed—his kind of love.

Looking back, I see how some particularly influential and unhappy people—people unable to give or receive the love they desperately wanted—altered my childhood. I also see how the bent love they showed me shaped what I believed about myself, family, and love itself. Watching for so many years and being wounded so many times, the brokenness of love impacted me forcefully. I grew up confused in many ways, trying to love but not knowing how.

As a child, I had a front-row seat for a parade of controlling and jealous romantic relationships. I thought that was normal, so I treated my boyfriends that way. When I got bored with a guy, I moved on to someone more exciting . . . at least for a while. Then, when I got restless again, I found someone else. No matter how many men I flirted with or dated, I never felt happy or satisfied. I kept searching, kept trying again, kept failing.

Partying on the weekends, wearing revealing clothes to get attention from men, and using money to impress or keep friends only made the emptiness inside me grow deeper and darker.

Whether they realize it or not, the people around us constantly teach us about love. This is especially true of our family members. Even if your biological parents played no part in your life, their lack of example formed you. The patterns established in our homes lead to hopefulness heartache. In my hurt, I questioned whether life had meaning or purpose. I had no respect for myself or others. I wanted love, but I had a false—or maybe I should say a corrupt—view of love.

What was your experience of love growing up?

For some of you reading this book, the story I've shared is unfathomable. You may have grown up feeling cherished and chosen, and I am so glad for you, sister. I mean that. What a gift you've been given.

It's possible that you grew up with a mixed bag when it comes to love. Maybe you hated your parents' divorce, but you ended up with a great stepparent. Maybe you had amazing siblings who filled you with love. Friends or church members or extended family members may have loved you deeply. Even with these great gifts, however, you may have grown up confused and heartbroken. Perhaps, like me, you've struggled to understand love because of what you've seen or experienced.

Wherever you're at, I pray you'll listen to the words of our heavenly Father: "'Though the mountains be shaken and the hills be removed, yet my unfailing love for you will not be shaken nor my covenant of peace be removed,' says the Lord, who has compassion on you" (Isa. 54:10). Beloved one, let this sink into your heart. To help truth take root in you, please reread that verse out loud, inserting your name wherever the word "you" appears. This is God's truth for you and for me!

God's unfailing love for you will never be shaken, and his covenant of peace will never be removed, says your Savior and King, who has compassion on you. His love for you will not fail. His peace will not be taken from you. His mercies for you will never end. I know it's difficult to believe this if your primary examples in childhood displayed little or no love. I hurt with you. I also urge you to open your heart to the possibility that you are loved enough by God that life can be different.

No matter where you've been or where you are currently, I invite you to lay any hurts from your past at the feet of Jesus right here, right now. I know reading this chapter won't solve all your pain, but I pray that as you read these words, you'll be able to enter into the Father's love for you—a love that will never change, never fail, never betray.

Begin at the Beginning

Being around an incredibly loving person is like drinking from the purest stream of water, eating the most delicious meal, hearing music so stunning it brings tears to your eyes. Or something like that. It's difficult even to describe love in all its richness and power. Sometimes we ache for love so much that it physically hurts. On the other hand, when we feel truly loved, we experience moments of peace and wholeness that we wish would last forever.

I imagine this is what Mary must have experienced the night she sat at Jesus's feet, hanging on his every word. As compelling as a teacher might be, it's not usually their knowledge that captivates us. It's love. Mary understood that she was loved enough that she could stop and simply *be*. Maybe Martha also understood that and simply got off track for a night. Or maybe she didn't understand the "completely enough" kind of love Jesus offered. Her motives don't interest me as much as what you and I do *with* the story.

We are not told every detail about Mary's and Martha's hearts. We speculate about their motives, their lifestyles, and their choices. And I'm sure that some of our assumptions tell a portion of the truth about these sisters and how our lives resemble theirs. It's important, however, that when we speak about what it means to be loved enough that our entire life becomes transformed by Love himself, that we don't inappropriately judge our sisters—either ancient or modern—who have different personalities than we do.

An active and busy woman who cooks, cleans, and hosts with great skill may be no less loving than a woman who sits on the couch listening to a friend's heartache. Remember, God has given each of us different gifts; perhaps the busy woman today will be the quiet listening woman tomorrow. As we've already discussed in our journey together, it's the posture of our hearts that God addresses.

This then leads us to ask, How do we posture our hearts so that we can love as the Father has loved us? How do we show genuine love rather than trying to get love through what we do or say? How do we authentically love without inappropriately judging or controlling our brothers and sisters in Christ, instead allowing God to work and display love in their hearts as he sees fit?

I believe all of this begins with understanding the Father's love for us. Without a true knowledge and heart experience of God's love, we will not be able to receive or offer love to others. We must begin at the beginning if we're to get anywhere at all.

Romans 5:8 provides a clear picture of what perfect love looks like: "God demonstrates his own love for us in this: While we were still sinners, Christ died for us." Love lays down his life for us without any expectation of getting something from us in return. Jesus didn't go to the cross because we were good; he suffered and died because, without his love, we would have remained enemies of truth and grace forever. We cannot earn this love, nor do we deserve it. "For the wages of sin is death," Romans 6:23 affirms, "but the free gift of God is eternal life in Christ Jesus our Lord."

God's love is free to us but cost him everything. Jesus bled in agony so that we could live freely and abundantly. How can we possibly receive, let alone return, such love?

Gratefully, love is not simply a thing God gives. Love is who our heavenly Father *is*. The apostle John emphasizes this point, and how it connects to our love for others, in a powerful way: "Dear friends, let us love one another, for love comes from God. Everyone who loves has been born of God and knows God. Whoever does not love does not know God, because God is love" (1 John 4:7–8). God *is* love, and those who know God love one another. Simple, certainly, but not always easy.

Fortunately, John helps us see how we can understand the Lord's love, return it in worship, and offer it to others: "We know how much God loves us, and we have put our trust in his love. God is love, and all who live in love live in God, and God lives in them. And as we live in God, our love grows more perfect" (1 John 4:16–17 NLT).

Putting our trust in God's love—relying on his love rather than our own efforts or feelings—allows us to love God and others in a deeper, truer way. And this is only possible through the indwelling of the Holy Spirit, who lives in us, as affirmed in these verses from 1 John and in Romans 8:11. With time, practice, and discipline, our love grows more perfect. What a beautiful promise, especially for those of us who grew up with few, if any, examples of authentic love. God, who *is* love, teaches us patiently and perfectly.

If you don't know how to love, if you feel as if the love you receive is never enough, if you long for a love that won't fail, place your trust in God's love alone. Don't look for love in relationships, money, success, or even happiness, though all of these may be given by God for your enjoyment.

And even if you've experienced the great gift of love from others while growing up, or through a wonderful marriage, or through godly friends, God still calls you to rely on his love alone. All gifts reflect the generous, lavish love of the Giver, your heavenly Father.

It's tempting to believe that the love we receive from others makes us enough, but don't fall into this trap set by the enemy of our souls. His plan is to "steal and kill and destroy" (John 10:10). He wants to destroy your relationships by leading you to rely too heavily on love from others to prove your worth, but your worth is not based on human love. He wants to steal your joy by keeping you in bondage to lies you may have heard all your life: *No one will ever love you. You'd better do [fill in the blank] if you want someone to care.*

Dearly beloved and set-apart daughter of God, these are lies from the enemy, arrows aimed directly at your heart.

Satan wants to kill your spirit, to keep you constantly questioning your belovedness. Don't listen to his lies!

In contrast to his description of the enemy, our Lord Jesus says of himself in the last words of John 10:10, "I have come that they may have life, and have it *to the full.*"

If you want to settle—once and for all—whether you are loved enough, you must begin at the beginning: "We love because he first loved us" (1 John 4:19). We've just seen that the love of our Father rescues us. Remember, while we were sinners, at war with God in our hearts, he died for us. Hallelujah forever! His love is free to us, though it cost him everything. (Need a reminder? Go back and read Romans 6:23.) Love is his identity, not just a resource he shares, and we can rely on this love . . . always.

Knowing these truths about the Father's love equips us in so many ways. Because God *is* love and we are called to be like God, love is first and foremost a part of our identity, not simply something we do. Filled with the Spirit of God, we love others as Love himself flows through us. How powerful is that? And what a relief it is that we don't have to manufacture love when we don't feel it. We can rely on God to love others through us.

Don't misunderstand me. Sins such as pride, anger, and selfishness can definitely block the flow of God's love from our hearts. But when we abide in Christ, as we're invited to do, his love overcomes our sin and reaches out to others. In a fascinating turn, we begin to see that loving others in the power of God helps us to believe more completely in our belovedness. Where once we might have looked to others to fill our love tank, in growing closer to Jesus—Love himself—we realize that we're already full. In fact, we have more than enough love in him. Our hearts can be settled and at peace, relying on Jesus's love and our enoughness in him.

However, because we are human and so prone to wander, we must keep vigilant watch over our hearts, which the book of Proverbs identifies as the wellspring of life. "Above all else, guard your heart, for everything you do flows from it" (Prov. 4:23). Let's turn our attention to some practical ways we can guard our hearts, remaining in and relying on God's love for our identity, peace, and strength.

On Guard

Growing up in the synagogue where they encountered the weekly reading of God's Word, Mary and Martha would have heard a great deal from the ancient book of wisdom called Proverbs. I imagine them listening to their rabbi read Proverbs 4:23 aloud: "Above all else, guard your heart, for everything you do flows from it."

Above all else . . .

Those are powerful, inciting words. I like to imagine Mary thinking about such words when she chose to sit at Jesus's feet rather than jumping up to help with the cooking and cleaning. And that evening Martha must have been confused about the way God wants us to show love toward others. The Word of God never says, "Watch over your reputation above all else; everyone will judge you otherwise." It doesn't say, "If you love people, you better impress them with your giftedness. Everything will fall into place if you succeed."

So many of us have believed lies like that at some point, but when we compare them to the truth of God's Word, it's pretty startling: "Above all else, guard your *heart*, for everything you do flows from it." Jesus spoke gently but firmly to his followers: "By this everyone will know that you are my disciples, if you love one another" (John 13:35). Again, not by how much or how well we do in life, not by how gifted we are, not by our perfect understanding of every Bible verse, but *by our love.*

So how do we protect our love and keep first things first by guarding our hearts? I propose seven ways, and as a memory aid, I've organized them all to begin with the letter *D.* If you wish to guard your heart, from which everything flows, watch your . . .

- **Desires.** Ask yourself, "What is my heart hungry for?" If your hunger for Jesus is strongest, you will not look to other people or things to settle the question of your belovedness.
- **Delights.** If you find that your chief delights in life don't line up with the Lord's will for you, pray about it. He will help you to "taste and see" that he is good (Ps. 34:8). John Piper says, "Pray that God will give you new taste buds on the tongue of your heart."[1]
- **Dependence.** Begin each morning by asking God to reveal where your heart is naturally bending. Maybe it's straight toward your phone. Perhaps it's to a person. It may be toward food or working out. Pray that the Lord will give you the humility and strength to abide first and most consistently in him (see John 15:1–17 for more on this).
- **Discernment.** Ask God to equip you to distinguish between good and evil. In Deuteronomy 30:19–20, God

makes a bold statement: "I have set before you life and death, blessings and curses. Now choose life, so that you and your children may live and that you may love the LORD your God, listen to his voice, and hold fast to him. For the LORD is your life." It seems like a no-brainer when God puts it this way. Who would choose death and curses? And yet we so often do! We need discernment to help us distinguish between good and evil, between God's love and lesser loves.

- **Desperation.** A heart desperate for God will not run after the things of this world or the lesser loves that can never fill us, such as relationships, accomplishments, and appearances. May our desperation for God's love alone increase.

- **Discipline.** Many people believe that love and discipline are incompatible, but that's not what the Bible teaches. Rather than despising discipline, we need to cultivate hearts that embrace it. Read Hebrews 12 for help with this, and pray for a heart strengthened by loving discipline.

- **Diligence.** If idle hands are the devil's playground, as the old saying goes, determine that diligence will mark your love for God and others. We don't earn God's love or seek affirmation from others by being diligent; instead, we honor God's lavish love by responding with cheerful and grateful hearts for the meaningful work he's called us to do (see Eph. 2:10).

What will it look like for you to pray about these seven Ds and seek to live them out? You will become more loving moment by moment. You'll choose generosity over greed, humility over pride, gratitude over discontentment, faithfulness over fruitlessness. If you ask me, that's a life worth living and a love worth showing!

As you seek to implement these seven Ds, remember that all of this begins and ends with God's unfailing love. I encourage you to meditate on and start to memorize one of the most beautiful passages about God's lavish love:

> How priceless is your unfailing love, O God!
>   People take refuge in the shadow of your wings.
> They feast on the abundance of your house;
>   you give them drink from your river of delights.
> For with you is the fountain of life;
>   in your light we see light. (Ps. 36:7–9)

A Viral Love Story

No matter where we come from, we can all learn to love God and one another more authentically. So I'd like to highlight three specific ways Christian women can grow in love: through vulnerable fellowship, godly service, and marriage and parenting. Of course, there are so many other ways we can learn to love, but just getting started with the basics in these three areas may be a huge challenge. Let's start by looking at love in one of the most unlikely places: the COVID-19 crisis.

Though my family, like yours, experienced great difficulty during the coronavirus pandemic of 2020, we also learned an amazing lesson about love. During yet another virtual Bible study, when all we wanted to do was fellowship in person, Rashawn and I shared vulnerably about the challenges we were facing sheltering in place with two babies and no family nearby. We needed prayer! Our group interceded for us so powerfully, and we definitely felt God's love through them.

A few days later, while Rashawn and I were sitting on our porch with the boys—not doing a whole lot but sick of being stuck inside all week—our oldest, Aiden, started running toward the street. I hopped up to chase him, scooped him into my arms, and noticed some friends parked a few houses away.

Huh. That's odd.

Then I saw more friends in their cars. Our fellowship group had gathered to surprise us with drive-by love—balloons (of course our boys were over the moon about those), food (one of my husband's love languages!), and a basket of spa goodies (aww . . . now *that* will do my body good!).

We were so humbled and grateful. Our friends stood in our driveway and affirmed the things God had done through us. They prayed for us so beautifully.

How crazy that the COVID-19 crisis taught me more powerfully than ever about giving and receiving love through fellowship. If you desire to receive and give love, I urge you to lean into fellowship. It takes time to build the kinds of relationships where people know and love one another on a deep level, so why not start—or continue—today!

In addition to fellowship, service is another significant way we give and receive love.

A Bowlful of Love

I'm used to serving others, and I enjoy serving others. It's easier for me to be on the demonstrating end of the love equation than the humbly receiving end. But God calls us to both. If you receive more love than you give, why not consider serving someone in love today. If you're a busy gal who offers, offers, offers, it may be time to let God love you through others.

I once learned this when I got sick while thousands of miles from home. Yeah, not ideal. Here's the backstory: Rashawn and I have traveled to the Philippines several times to serve, share the gospel with, and learn from the Philippine people. On one trip, however, I could do nothing for several days.

Spiking a high fever and so weak that getting up felt impossible, I lay in bed wondering why God brought us halfway around the world only for me to be so sick. Honestly, all I wanted was water, soup, and fruit. I had no idea how to get those things, though. There were no convenience stores, let alone giant grocery chains, in the Philippine town where we were serving. Sister, I lay there feeling pretty down.

Lo and behold, a gentle knock on the door and a kind voice brought me out of a fevered daze. A sister in Christ had come and brought me—I kid you not—homemade chicken soup, a plate of fruit, and a large bottle of water. I had never in my life felt so seen by my heavenly Father and so loved by a stranger, someone I thought I had come to serve.

Whatever she put in that soup (I'm guessing a whole lotta love), it nourished me so much that I was able to rejoin the team the next day. Over the next several days, I watched as that woman took care of her family and served others. She did everything with such a beautiful heart for God, and it was clear she felt joyful and loved as she served.

On that trip I learned how service can be a huge way that we both give and receive love. Sometimes we think we'll just be drained by service, but the opposite is true in God's economy. When we serve in reliance on God's love as we're commanded to in 1 John 4:7–12, we receive so much love in return. Our love tank becomes fuller as we serve from a heart overflowing with God's love.

What Princesses Don't Know

Before we close this chapter on love, I'd like to touch on the love we learn in marriage and parenting. I know that not all the women reading this book are married, and some of you who are married may not have children. Others may have a gaggle of kiddos. Some of you have lost husbands and children. Family life—and the love that's supposed to come with it—can actually hurt . . . so much. Wherever we're at, we can all learn or be reminded about love in marriage and parenting.

Literally hundreds of books have been written about this subject, so this one small section won't be able to address all the complexities that make married love and parenting so rich and challenging. I simply want to point out one way in which many women develop a false understanding about love and then offer a suggestion for how we can move beyond that in the true love of Christ.

Like many of you, the fairy tales I watched or read as a child set me up to believe that I'd fall in love, that I'd be rescued by love, and that love would be happily ever after if I could just find the right guy (usually a prince).

Sister, these things did not prepare me for the kind of love God tells me should mark marriage and parenting: "Love is patient, love is kind. It does not envy, it does not boast, it is not proud. It does not dishonor others, it is not self-seeking, it is not easily angered, it keeps no record of wrongs. Love does not delight in evil but rejoices with the truth. It always protects, always trusts, always hopes, always perseveres. Love never fails" (1 Cor. 13:4–8).

The kind of love God calls us to show in marriage and child-raising is far from a fairy-tale kind of love. For some of us, that can be a disappointing message, but only if we're looking to the love of a spouse or children to fill us, to make us feel like we're enough. Remember, if we rely on God and abide in the richness of his unfailing love, we won't *need* others to love us perfectly. Sure, we'll get to enjoy the love they offer us, but we won't be disappointed when their love is as imperfect as the love we show them.

Here's the secret to love that no fairy-tale princess seems to understand: we are called to encourage our husbands and children to place their hope in God's love alone and to model that for them. As we do, we reaffirm that God is love, and his love never fails. Whether you're married or not, whether you have children or not, decide today that you'll love others through Love himself.

I know we've only scratched the surface when it comes to learning love through fellowship, service, and family. There's so much more, so stay tuned! In the chapters to come, we'll be using what we learned here as a springboard to help us grow even more. Before we press on, however, let me pray for you, beloved one, that the truths about God's unfailing love might take root deep within you.

Heavenly Father, *thank you for your mercy. Thank you for loving us in a way no one else can. Thank you for showing us what true love is, for pouring out that love on us by shedding your precious blood on the cross for our sins so that we can have relationship with you. I pray over my sister reading this book right now, Lord. Maybe she didn't feel loved growing up. Maybe she doesn't feel loved right now. Father, I ask that you would pour out your unconditional love over her, that she would tangibly feel your presence and your heart for her. I pray she would receive your love and spread it to others. In Jesus's name, amen.*

9

SET APART
AND FULLY KNOWN

I REALIZE NOW how differently my story could have gone.

Realistically, every one of us can say that. God alone knows all the ways in which he's protected and guided us. Looking back, however, I see how easily things could have turned out for the worse. Rashawn and I met online, we dated long-distance for six months before getting engaged, then we married a week later and I moved halfway across the country to start my new life as his wife. I was following the leading of the Lord the best I knew how, and I believed that his will for my life included Rashawn. Getting to know him has been one of the most wonderful gifts God's ever given me.

It didn't take me long to realize, though, that I knew very little about my new husband. Thankfully, the more time I spent with Rashawn, the more I grew to love him. We faced challenges, just like any other couple learning to love each other; there have been tough times, sister! But I've seen so clearly that knowing and loving any person includes being willing to study them, to invest time in getting to know what they like and don't like, why they do what they do, what motivates their thoughts and actions. I decided early on to commit to this in my marriage, and our relationship has grown as a result. By the grace of God, our story of knowing and loving each other continues in joy to this day.

I also know that some stories end in heartache, betrayal, and divorce. Getting to know another person can hurt, can't it? So can being known by others.

Human relationships are complicated. We may think we know someone and then discover we've only scratched the surface of how wonderful they truly are. Other times we find out a friend, family member, or significant other posed and postured and presented themselves in false ways.

And allowing ourselves to be known is no less complex. How tempting it is to hide the parts of us that we're unsure about or ashamed of, to present ourselves in a way that we think will make us more lovable. I'll say it again: knowing people—and being known by them—is *so* complicated!

What tremendous relief and peace it can give us to acknowledge the all-knowing and all-loving nature of our God. When Jesus walked on earth, we're told that "he knew all people" (John 2:24). The original Greek word used here indicates our Lord knew every detail of people's hearts.[1] There was no keeping secrets from him. Nothing was hidden from him; he understood people completely. That means Jesus understood every single ugly thing about us when he lovingly, willingly laid down his life for us. How amazing is that? How grateful I am! With God, knowing and loving are inseparable. To be known by God is to be loved by God. To be loved by him is to be known by him.

Many women find this tough to understand. Maybe you grew up thinking if people *really* knew you, there's no chance they would love you. People may have actually said things like that to you, or they may have communicated that to you through their actions. Dear sister, I am so, so sorry if this was your experience.

For other women, the pain of getting to know people and finding out they weren't who they claimed to be has soured the idea that knowing and loving always go together. It may be what God intended, but your experience screams otherwise, and it's difficult for you to imagine how knowing others and being known by them could lead you into greater love.

In other words, people reading this book will have radically different experiences with knowing and being known. Because of that, I want us to look at how and why God designed knowing and loving. No matter where we've been in the past, let's link arms today, going together to the place God is calling us.

Eden Equals . . .

The book of Genesis is a book of beginnings. That's what the word "genesis" actually means—the start, the origin, the beginning. What we find at the very beginning of the human story is incredible closeness between God and Adam and Eve, the man and woman he created to reflect his image. Nothing separated the Creator and his creation in the world's first garden. The name of this garden, Eden, is a Hebrew word that can mean delight, pleasure, or paradise. To put this all together, at the beginning of our human story is total delight in God, pleasure in knowing him and being known by him, and the enjoyment of his perfect paradise on earth.

But we know things didn't stay in this state of perfection. Into the garden of Eden slithered Satan, God's enemy, who lied to Eve and led her to question God.

> He said to the woman, "Did God really say, 'You must not eat from any tree in the garden?'"
>
> The woman said to the serpent, "We may eat fruit from the trees in the garden, but God did say, 'You must not eat fruit from the tree that is in the middle of the garden, and you must not touch it, or you will die.'"
>
> "You will not certainly die," the serpent said to the woman. "For God knows that when you eat from it your eyes will be opened, and you will be like God, knowing good and evil." (Gen. 3:1–5)

If you ask me, it's pretty fascinating that the first sin involved knowing. Satan tempts our first mother with fruit from the tree of the knowledge of good and evil, which God had told Adam and Eve would lead to death, "for when you eat from it you will certainly die" (Gen. 2:17).

What we have here is a crazy situation. Adam and Eve had been created by a God who loved them and attended to their every need, including the need to be known and loved by one another. The Lord saw it was not good for the man to be alone (Gen. 2:18), so he provided relationship, the chance to know and be known. When God brought Adam and Eve together, he blessed human knowing. But here's the crazy thing: being known and loved by God and by Adam didn't feel like enough for Eve. She longed to know more. What she didn't understand was that the knowledge the enemy offered her wasn't a gift or a means of empowerment; it was *death*. The Genesis account shows us that sin introduced death, brokenness, shame, and fear into our world.

True love enables us to be known and safe. This was God's original intention for us, and it is his perfect plan for all eternity, when Jesus returns to sit on his throne and sin and death finally pass away. For the time being, though, sin fills our knowing with brokenness and hurt.

I'm so grateful God did not leave us in our sin. "As a father has compassion on his children, so the LORD has compassion on those who fear him; for he *knows* how we are formed, he *remembers* that we are dust" (Ps. 103:13–14). He knows. He remembers creating us from the dust and breathing into us the gift of life. He laid down his own life as a bridge between the brokenness of our beginning and the final glory of our end. "For God so loved the world that he gave his one and only Son, that whoever believes in him shall not perish but have eternal life" (John 3:16). Jesus knows us and he loves us. He knows us and he rescues us. He knows us and he makes it possible for us to know him too.

This deep, inescapable knowing and being known by God honestly scares some people. "Death and Destruction lie open before the LORD—how much more do human hearts!" (Prov. 15:11). Having no secrets from God may make you feel uneasy. That's totally understandable. As humans, we're used to hiding parts of ourselves that we don't like, aren't we? That also goes all the way back to the garden, when Adam and Eve knew they were naked, felt

the shame of their sin, and hid from their beloved Creator
(Gen. 3:7–10).

I'm so grateful we don't have to stay in that place of hiding. Psalm 139 teaches us that God's perfect knowing—his
no-secrets love—is a priceless gift. In Psalm 139:17 David
exclaims, "How precious to me are your thoughts, God!"
This follows an amazing and beautiful description of how
God knows us. I invite you to read these verses slowly, relishing the truth of each image and statement:

> You have searched me, LORD,
> and you know me.
> You know when I sit and when I rise;
> you perceive my thoughts from afar.
> You discern my going out and my lying down;
> you are familiar with all my ways.
> Before a word is on my tongue
> you, LORD, know it completely.
> You hem me in behind and before,
> and you lay your hand upon me.
> Such knowledge is too wonderful for me,
> too lofty for me to attain.
>
> Where can I go from your Spirit?
> Where can I flee from your presence?
> If I go up to the heavens, you are there;
> if I make my bed in the depths, you are there.
> If I rise on the wings of the dawn,
> if I settle on the far side of the sea,
> even there your hand will guide me,
> your right hand will hold me fast.
> If I say, "Surely the darkness will hide me
> and the light become night around me,"

> even the darkness will not be dark to you;
> > the night will shine like the day,
> > for darkness is as light to you. (Ps. 139:1–12)

"Such knowledge is too wonderful for [us]." How true is that? God's love and knowledge are both exciting and exposing. But, dear sister, there is *freedom* in being fully known by God. Psalm 139 makes this completely clear. He knows every detail of our lives. There is nothing hidden from him—not a thought, an emotion, a twitch in your eye. He knows and sees absolutely everything about you. And in that perfect knowing, he promises to love you and never forsake you. Even the darkness of our hearts is as light to him (v. 12). Hallelujah!

God isn't going to walk out after getting to know you because he decides you're not worth the effort. God isn't going to stop loving you because of what you've done . . . ever. He promises, "'Never will I leave you; never will I forsake you.' . . . So we say with confidence, 'The Lord is my helper; I will not be afraid. What can mere mortals do to me?' . . . Jesus Christ is the same yesterday and today and forever" (Heb. 13:5–6, 8). God's love for you doesn't change with knowing; it's *based* in knowing. How good is that news?

At the root of our desire to be known and loved is our original created design. God made us to be known and loved at the same time. Knowledge without love doesn't work. First Corinthians 8 teaches this clearly: "Knowledge puffs up while love builds up. Those who think they know something do not yet know as they ought to know. But whoever loves God is known by God" (vv. 1–3). Love without knowledge also doesn't work. Such "love" bends and twists with every trial, and hardship may break it altogether.

When united, however, God's love and knowledge provide us with perfect confidence and security. From the very beginning until the very end, we're fully known and loved by him.

I get that this is a huge concept to grasp, but it's also the starting point for so much else. Don't just take my word for it; keep pressing into God's truth that you are fully known and fully loved. I've recommended a couple of online resources in the endnotes to help you.[2] While we continue to grow in this area, let's also look at other dynamics of knowing and loving. I want to turn our attention first to how we know ourselves.

What Type Are You?

I wonder how Mary and Martha would score if they took a personality or self-awareness test. There are actually quite a few predictions available online about these two sisters' personality types. Some people try to better understand Mary and Martha through a number or a group of letters or a StrengthsFinder profile. In other words, lots of people are interested in classifying and categorizing Mary and Martha in ways that help us know them better. People can go crazy doing this for their own personalities too.

Self-awareness has been a buzzword for some time now; personality testing or profiling is all the rage. And while it's impossible to know exactly how Mary or Martha would score on any given test, there seems no shortage of ways we can "know ourselves" better. The number of internet personality tests alone that are available every minute of every day can be overwhelming.

Some people pay hundreds of dollars for professional personality tests that promise to help us know ourselves better. Others take endless free online quizzes that tell which character from their favorite film they're most like or which British royal shares their personality. While these can be good fun, you and I both know they are kind of a waste of time. Do I really need to know if my personality type is the same as the queen or princess of a country I've never visited? Probably not.

But as God's set-apart daughters, is it important for us to know ourselves? Absolutely.

As we've already discussed and seen revealed through many Bible verses, God has inseparably connected knowing and loving. We can't love ourselves without knowing ourselves, and we can't know ourselves without trusting we are loved and fully embracing our identity as beloved daughters. As helpful as personality profiles may be, no test result can convince us of the truth that we are fully known and fully loved by God. Only closeness with our Creator through prayer and reading his Word can do that.

Personality profiling may be beneficial if you already believe that you are fully known and loved and are set apart for God's perfect purposes. Without that foundation, though, knowing and loving can actually become more confusing. I'm concerned that some of us look to online tests not only to tell us who we are but also to tell everyone else how they should interact with us. You may have seen social media posts like this: "I'm a [insert personality type here]. That's why I do this or feel that. If you want to love me, you should . . ."

Risen Motherhood, a great podcast from one of my favorite online communities, helped me think through this. In one episode, as a conversation unfolded between the hosts about being known by God, knowing ourselves, and longing to be understood by others, Laura Wilfer made this excellent point:

> We see that this [wanting knowledge] is really nothing new. Eve did this when she took a bite of the fruit. She wanted knowledge. She walked with the source of all knowledge; she could've asked God absolutely *anything,* but she wanted to be in control, have the power, and be able to wield it at her own whims. I think we do this same thing Eve did when we believe if we know our personality test, understand how we work and what makes us tick, we'll gain knowledge to help us control our lives.[3]

Knowing ourselves and being known by others is so important, but *not* so we can control our lives or the lives of others. Any external means of knowing ourselves have to be built on the foundation of our identity in Christ, the set-apart belovedness we've been looking at throughout this book.

Imagine if Martha had said to Jesus, "Lord, I hear what you're saying, but I'm a 2 (or an ENFP, or [fill in the blank]). You know it's impossible for me to slow down. This is who I am. Mary should know that." Kinda crazy to imagine that, isn't it? Yet that's often how personality profiles and tests are used—as a weapon of supposed self-knowledge that no one can argue against.

Yes, we have been created with certain temperaments. Yes, personality tests can help us understand ourselves. No control or power comes with that, though. Instead, our reaction to self-knowledge of any kind should be humility before God and gratitude for his all-knowing, all-loving nature.

One of the most beautiful and wildest things about falling in love with Jesus is this: the more we know him, the more we come to know ourselves. He literally formed us. He knows everything about us. Seems pretty obvious that he'd be the best source of information about us, doesn't it? If you want to understand yourself, go to Jesus. When you do, he will help you. John Piper describes it this way:

> Over time, in proportion to what is good for you, he will begin to lay you bare, and you will begin to gain some measure of self-understanding. And in heaven it will be complete, and you will be completely purified so you won't be as devastated as you would be if you knew yourself completely here. He [Jesus] knows what we can handle, and it is glorious to know that we are known by one who can help us know ourselves. . . . [It's] good news to be known to the bottom of your being.[4]

Amen to that!

I hope you can see that not only are knowing and loving tied together by God, but also that knowing yourself is inseparably tied to being known and loved by God. It all fits together.

As we grow in these areas, we also realize that what we're known for forms another piece of the knowing and loving puzzle. So let me ask you: What are you currently known for? What do you *want* to be known for? Let's look at these things next.

For the Kingdom's Sake

A few years back, when we were married without children, I had a desire to do something big for God. I wanted to change the world. How? I had no idea. All I knew was that I wanted to do something powerful for the kingdom.

Over time, a desire to go overseas and share the good news and love of Jesus flooded my heart. Now I knew . . . I wanted to be a missionary. I filled out various applications to go overseas on short-term mission trips. I wanted to be known as a kingdom builder.

Of course I thought God would bless this plan. So when things didn't work out financially and I was told that I needed to be married at least a year before I could be considered by the mission agencies, I was devastated and discouraged. I wanted to make an impact in people's lives, especially in the lives of those who were poor and needy. I wanted to do that for the sake of the gospel.

In my frustration, I began to grumble. *Why wouldn't you want me to help others and share your love with everyone, Lord?* I wanted to experience sharing the gospel with people face-to-face. I wanted to know what serving day in and day out really looked like. My husband was traveling to Israel, but I had nowhere to go but home. It seemed like everyone else who loved Jesus was able to do great things for the kingdom. Why not me?

Did you catch how much "I" and "me" was involved there? In some ways, my motives had deceived me. I wanted to be known and loved as a woman of God, but I had confused doing something "big" for God's kingdom with his perfect plan for my life. I wanted to be known for the way I loved others and how much I traveled to spread the Good News.

God wanted me to be known and loved in his way and in his time. As I've already shared with you, I wasn't raised in a Christ-centered home, and I had a lot of growing to do in my faith. I needed to learn how to love and serve others out of my identity in Christ. Even though I thought I was ready to do huge things for his kingdom, during that time God showed me that I needed to be known and loved by him first.

I also needed to know myself as his daughter, as a wife, as a friend, and eventually as a mama. I had to go through life in Christ and experience the suffering that comes with it in order to truly understand the struggles and brokenness others face. This helped me begin learning to know and love others as Jesus knows and loves me. It also helped me become known for his work in my life, not for what I wanted to do for him.

Sometimes ambition and inauthenticity can get mixed up with our Christian life. We all want to be known and loved, and most of us want others to know and love us for the cool things we do or for how our lives look. If this wasn't true, none of us would be on social media. We want people to see us in certain ways, to know and love the parts of us that we want to share. We also want them to *not* know certain things, mostly because we fear that being known in this way would result in being loved less.

Wanting to do wonderful things for God's kingdom and wanting to be known for doing his work can be good desires, but if our hearts are filled with striving and posing, trouble's brewing. Rashawn and I watched this with a brother in Christ.

This beloved one was very zealous for the kingdom of God. He always wanted bigger, better, and more, but always "for the kingdom." Let me tell you . . . he had a *lot* of things going for the sake of God: a business, a successful blog, a beautiful family, a nice house in the city center, and a stable income he could use for ministry.

But over time, Rashawn and I began to notice some concerning things. The more projects this friend took on for God's kingdom, the more goals he set, the more he went after the next thing and the "best of the best" for Christ's sake, the more tense and weary he became. I started to wonder . . . what's really driving him? At some point, our brother in Christ had become more ambitious than dependent on the Holy Spirit.

Instead of becoming known for his work for God's kingdom, people started knowing him as the guy who didn't spend time with his family, the guy who easily got irritable and frustrated when his plans didn't succeed. Honestly, he experienced burnout like I had never seen. He had become so caught up in doing things for God that he completely missed what the kingdom is all about.

We are called to be known and loved by God and to know and love him. We are called to be known and loved by others and to give back that knowing and loving to the people around us. We may also wish to be known as an excellent business owner, a spiritual woman, a godly wife or mother. And while it's certainly not sinful to be recognized for our professionalism or our spiritual giftedness, when we focus on such things more than our identity in Christ, we're in dangerous waters.

I wonder what Mary and Martha wanted to be known for. Did Martha want to impress Jesus with her giftedness as a host? Did she want to be known by others as the woman who served Christ the best dinner in the cleanest house? We'll never know for certain, but I confess that I've wanted to be known for things other than my identity as God's beloved. At different points I've wanted to be known for being pretty or for having an amazing family or for being the hardest worker or for doing the biggest things for God.

What have you wanted to be known for? Maybe you've never wanted to do something big, but has your heart ever longed to be loved or known for something? No matter how big or small our plans are, if we want to be known and loved for anything we do, for anything we are apart from being God's beloved daughter, we'll run into hurt and disappointment.

A woman who is confident in her set-apart identity in Christ doesn't strive. She'll be known for living out her calling and giftedness in a posture of humility. This is why Jesus reminded Martha that the better part is closeness to him, not scurrying here, there, and everywhere trying to *be* something. Sometimes the biggest and best thing we can do for God's kingdom—and for ourselves too—is to sit quietly at Jesus's feet.

It's so tempting to want to be the woman known for her passionate prayers or her super organized house or her DIY crafts or her well-behaved children who can recite Scripture anytime, anywhere. The trouble is that none of those things can take the place of what we are *always* known and admired for. Even the most well-behaved children have tantrums, our crafts may fail, someone inevitably messes up our clean house, and our spiritual gifts don't always look impressive. Only God's love never fails, as 1 Corinthians 13:8 promises.

Dear one, decide that you will be known and loved for one thing: your identity as a beloved daughter of the King.

When you make that choice day after day, everything else begins to fall into place. Because sin continues to tempt us, this isn't a "one and done" decision. We have to keep deciding to be known and loved by God, to know ourselves as his daughters, and to be known and loved by others for who we truly are in Jesus. This is a choice to be free, to be authentic, to know and love life. Doesn't that sound good?

Father, *we were created to be known and loved by you. You knew us when we were in our mothers' wombs, and you also know every detail of our lives. You know the struggles and anxieties that we carry. Because you know us so completely, we never walk alone, but we walk with you, Father. And I pray for my sister who is reading this book, that you would draw her close to you, that she would get to know you for who you are. Remind her that she is not known because of the things she does or does not do, but for who she is in you. Thank you for loving us, for seeing us, and for giving us new names. In Jesus's name, amen.*

10

SET APART
THROUGH HUMILITY

If you flew to Puerto Rico today, one of the first sounds you'd hear after exiting the airport would be horns honking. For many Puerto Ricans, driving their car without using its horn is unthinkable; the horn is like an extension of their emotions. People in PR literally talk to one another with their horns. Frustrated on the road? Honk. In a hurry? Honk. Someone takes .01 seconds too long at a stoplight? Honk, honk, honk.

Back in chapter 7, I described how impatient life in Puerto Rico can feel. People are working hard or socializing loudly, cleaning intently or driving fiercely. Giving other drivers the benefit of the doubt just isn't done. Rushed driving was the only kind of driving I learned; like everyone else, I was always in a hurry to get to the next thing. I knew best how people should drive and would use my horn to let them know it. But did I realize I lived this way prior to arriving in the United States? Not a chance.

In fact, I'm not even sure I fully recognized this until I married Rashawn. I certainly didn't think of myself as someone with road rage. After all, I was a nice Christian girl when I got married. At least I was . . . until someone cut me off without so much as flashing a blinker.

I vividly remember Rashawn and I getting on the road together one Tuesday evening around five o'clock. Rush-hour traffic, when everyone is desperate to get home, does not bring out the fruit of the Spirit in people. Self-control, patience, and joy don't typically flood the highways at that time.

Out of nowhere, a car pulled out in front of us. My husband slammed on his brakes, and adrenaline exploded into my veins. We were safe, thank God, but I let loose a tirade of words: "Who would do such a thing? I can't believe that guy even has a license! Why didn't you honk, Rashawn?"

My husband just sat quietly behind the wheel. Like many people in the US, Rashawn's first reaction isn't to use the car horn. Come to think of it, I wonder if some people here even know how to use their car's horn.

So fast-forward a bit. Now Rashawn and I have babies. A car jumps into our lane with no signal, and what do I do? I honk the horn *for* my husband. I mean, someone's got to do it. I have little ones in the car; there's no time for merciful driving.

That's when God convicted me of something: I had no grace for other drivers. I felt superior to them. Their mistakes were an inconvenience to me, and I was sure to let them know it. I was quick to honk and slow to be patient. Even though I wanted someone to be gracious with me when I got a bit distracted by one of my boys' needs at a stoplight, I didn't extend that same kindness to others. Pride made me believe I was a better driver than everyone else.

I use this example because it illustrates how insidious pride can be in our lives. Christian women don't usually brag about their bodies, houses, or vacations. In fact, we often put ourselves down in an "I'm nothing special, I'm just doing the best I can" sort of way. While we may not be overtly prideful, we can display a lack of humility in uniquely dangerous ways. For example, we sometimes place ourselves in a category above others—even in something as seemingly insignificant as driving skills—when God calls us to be gracious in *every* area.

Please don't misunderstand me here. I'm not saying that using your car's horn equals being prideful. Honking your horn when someone cuts you off can be the right thing to do in many situations. But using the horn in a prideful way—"I'm a better driver than you and I'm going to let you know it!"—chips away at an essential virtue Jesus invites us to cultivate.

God calls us all to practice humility. And many of us learn humility at work, in our relationships with our parents or siblings, and through marriage and parenting. But we can also learn humility in a zillion little things. Jesus has taught me humility on the road. When I'm behind the wheel, he asks me to extend grace to others.

In what areas of life is God calling you to learn humility?

That's a potentially uncomfortable question, isn't it? If you're anything like me, asking God to teach you patience and humility probably isn't the first prayer on your lips. But I'm not trying to pin you with guilt and shame about that. Truly! The struggle is real for me, so I'm preaching to the choir. As Jesus teaches me about humility, I'm simply inviting you on the journey. And I promise not to honk at you along the way.

Actually at His Feet

Have you ever heard certain Christian phrases and wondered how on earth you're supposed to live them out? For example, someone says, "Find your identity in Christ." Yes! I want that! How in the world do I do that? Or we're told, "Sit at the feet of Jesus." Yes! I've read that story, and I want what Mary had. What does it really mean to sit at Jesus's feet, though?

I got an incredible picture of this when our oldest son, Aiden, had just barely begun to walk. Hearing his dad's voice, Aiden toddled into the office where Rashawn was on a phone call. I watched as Aiden literally lay down at Rashawn's feet, content to simply listen to his father's voice. Aiden's greatest desire at that moment was just to be near his daddy. What a perfect illustration of humility.

In Luke 10, Mary took this same posture with Jesus. It's important to note, however, that it wasn't Mary's physical position that Jesus acknowledged. Again, it was Mary's heart that Jesus saw. Her heart's desire was to be near her Lord.

I firmly believe that if Martha had embraced a heart of humility while she finished up her work, the story in Luke 10 could have ended much differently. Perhaps Martha wouldn't have continued her work at all. Perhaps she would have joined her sister at Jesus's feet. And while we can't know "what might have been," we can learn from this story.

If you've ever wondered what sitting at Jesus's feet really looks like, cultivating humility is an essential place to start.

When we realize how big our God is and how truly small we are, humility is the natural result. In humility we recognize our limited capabilities. Humility reminds us not only that we can *not* do all things but also that we can control very little of what happens around us. Grasping God's amazing grace and almighty power fuels humility in us. When we have humble hearts, we understand and acknowledge that everything we possess—our abilities, gifts, resources . . . even our personalities—comes straight from the hand of God.

A humble woman gives glory to the One who supplies every need. A humble woman seeks honor for God, not for herself, and realizes that we can do nothing apart from Christ (see John 15:5). A humble heart willingly takes the lowest position, the position of service.

Perhaps this is why the world scorns humility. For many, humility equals weakness. Our culture insists that the confident, bold, strong woman gets the reward, not the meek, humble servant. Though the world might acknowledge a humble person as someone having a "good heart," most people in our culture don't see the value of humility when compared to the power and position that pride promises.

Biblical humility doesn't mean being weak or powerless, though. The Bible tells us that Jesus—the same Jesus who brought the dead back to life with matchless power—offers us the perfect example of humility. Though he was God incarnate, Jesus "did not come to be served, but to serve, and to give his life as a ransom for many" (Mark 10:45). At the same time, "The Son [Jesus] is the radiance of God's glory and the exact representation of his being, sustaining all things by his powerful word" (Heb. 1:3). Humility doesn't mean weakness; it recognizes and rightly exercises power but doesn't live for it.

So what did humility look like in Jesus's life? Our Lord generously gave himself away. He lived simply. He poured himself out, expecting nothing in return. He enjoyed the love of those around him, but he didn't practice humility to get something back. He knew his abilities but didn't seek glory for himself. In fact, Jesus addressed this straightforwardly: "Whoever speaks on their own does so to gain personal glory, but he who seeks the glory of the one who sent him is a man of truth; there is nothing false about him" (John 7:18).

Humility rewires our thinking. Instead of looking out for number one, we look to Jesus and look out for others. The apostle Paul urges, "Do nothing out of selfish ambition or vain conceit. Rather, in humility value others above yourselves, not looking to your own interests but each of you to the interest of others. In your relationships with one another, have the same mindset as Christ Jesus: Who, being in very nature God, did not consider equality with God something to be used to his own advantage; rather, he made himself nothing by taking the very nature of a servant" (Phil. 2:3–7).

Don't let the radical truth of this passage pass by you today. Jesus did not consider his calling or giftedness something to be grasped or used to his advantage. He made himself nothing and took on the very nature of a servant, and he did nothing out of selfish ambition, pride, or vanity. Wow! I am continually amazed at Jesus. What he did seems impossible. How can we ever live this way?

Thankfully, that same passage provides us with a starting point: "In your relationships with one another, have the same mindset as Christ Jesus" (v. 5). If you want to be humble like Jesus, start right where you are—at home, at work, at the grocery store, or in the car. Practice humility in your relationships first.

Personally, it's a lot easier to be humble during my quiet time than when someone gets in my way. In those "I'm not getting what I want" moments, humility can be so tough. Can you relate?

On Saturdays, Rashawn will often watch the boys so I can get some alone time. Inevitably, though, it seems like the Saturdays when I've got perfect plans and am most looking forward to "my time" are the ones when Rashawn is up and out of the house before I even open my eyes. My wants are threatened, and I'm left fighting rising annoyance. Did I inform Rashawn of my plans? No. Do I show him humility and grace, believing the best of my husband? Umm . . .

In situations like this, I'm challenged to humbly trust God to work out the details for my day, even if things don't start out just as I hoped. The temptation, though, is to put a wedge between Rashawn and myself because I didn't get my way. That's my pride, sister. It's the same pride that tempts me to believe I'm a better driver than others; it just shows up in a different way. I wonder if God told us to practice humility in our relationships because he knew that would be the very place we'd be most tempted by pride.

If, like me, you think you might have room to grow in humility, let's look at one specific way to put humility into practice in our daily relationships. Stick with me, sister, because this might surprise you.

Judge Much?

Growing up, I never wondered if my mom was a hard worker. Her diligence was obvious. Because Mom worked hard and put in long hours, my sister and I had the privilege of going to private school. We also spent a lot of time in daycare. I didn't question whether this was good or bad; it's just how things were. That's why, years later, it honestly would have made more sense to me if God had led me to work an eight-to-five job than to stay at home as a wife and mom.

No one forced me to stay home with Aiden and Eliyah, and I don't stay home because I feel guilt at the thought of having a job. Working motherhood was modeled for me growing up, and I always had jobs when I was single. Being a stay-at-home mom was a completely foreign idea to me, and when God called me to do that, it felt kind of scary. Rashawn and I weren't financially stable. We didn't have the kind of home or the resources we wanted. At the same time, the Holy Spirit's call was so strong that I honestly didn't consider rejecting it. It really came down to whether I trusted God or not. God wanted to cultivate humility in me by calling me to serve my husband and babies.

Let's pause for a moment of clarification. Am I telling you that every woman learns humility best by staying at home, keeping house, and caring for little ones? As the apostle Paul might say, by no means! Remember . . . we closed the last section by reflecting on how humility starts in our relationships. I share my story with you because I want us to think about how easy it is for us to judge one another in our various callings and forget humility as we do.

For women who stay at home, it can be tempting to believe they've chosen "what is better." For women who work, it may be tempting to think, "Believe me; this calling is a lot harder. Staying home doesn't take as much strength as being a working woman." A woman who has a public ministry may find it difficult to resist the temptation to view her calling as higher or more spiritual, while a woman who quietly, faithfully serves others at her local church or through prayer may look at others and think, "What I'm doing isn't good enough." No matter where we find ourselves, it's so easy to judge our sisters in Christ.

Humility helps us to see our calling accurately—as a path on which God sets us for *his* glory and *his* purposes. Humility is all about looking at Jesus, not at ourselves and not at others. We cultivate humility when, instead of passing judgment on our sisters in Christ, we allow God to develop our trust in and dependence on him.

I've had several family members actually ask me, "Why don't you work? Doesn't it bother you that you're not doing something with your life?" Whereas some Christian sisters feel pressure to stay at home, I've felt the opposite. Rather than listening to the "not enough" voices, I need to humbly follow God's calling for me. Beloved daughter of God, I urge you to do the same.

Jesus calls us to exercise humility before him and in how we look at others. We do this when we acknowledge that God's calling and giftedness are unique for each person. We can't know perfectly what God is calling someone else to do; it's difficult enough for us to stay in step with the Holy Spirit's call in our own life.

When we choose to humble ourselves in our calling, however, we can also humble ourselves in our giftedness. When we're confident in our call, we won't have to downplay or overplay our gifts and abilities; we can rejoice that they are given by God and that he allows us to use them. He gets all the glory when we rightly own our giftedness, which is as it should be!

A woman with a humble heart doesn't think less of herself and obsess about every little thing that's wrong. She spends her thoughts on God! She thinks of herself less often and deliberately celebrates the giftedness of others. She demonstrates true humility, not pride disguised with humble talk.

This brings up a difficult topic but one that's essential to address. In Christian circles, many of us learn to practice a false kind of humility. If we're to truly honor Christ with humble hearts, we not only need to stop judging others in their callings but also to stop acting humble in ways that are inauthentic.

To Be Is Better Than to Seem

I've discovered that it's most difficult for me to practice humility when others compliment me or point out my giftings. I remember welcoming a couple to our house for the first time; the wife immediately highlighted how beautiful our home was. My response was something like, "Oh, you're too kind; I'm just doing my best." This sounded good, but I'll be honest: I'm not sure if it was insecurity that caused me to say this or if I was trying to hide how proud I felt.

The pull of fake humility creates a real struggle for us as women. A lot of us don't even recognize that false humility can actually be pride in disguise. How does this look in real life? For women, it often comes out when we devalue ourselves or our gifts so that we look humble. We want to appear one way, when what's inside may be completely different; we may want to *seem* humble more than truly *be* humble. Deflecting recognition and praise, fishing for compliments, drawing attention to ourselves through so-called humblebragging and self-deprecating humor—these can all be ways Christian women fall into the trap of fake humility.[1]

Now, you may be thinking, "Hold on . . . don't those things actually prove a woman has low self-esteem?" Potentially, yes. But what looks like an inferiority complex, self-loathing, or the belief that "I'm less than others" can actually be a twisted form of pride. If humility is thinking of yourself less, not thinking less of yourself, then pride is thinking of yourself not only more highly than you ought but also more often than is healthy or holy.

True humility is *not* the same as low self-esteem, intense personal criticism, or insecurity in our own giftedness and enoughness. Those things are weights far too heavy to bear. God never meant for being ourselves to be a burden! Focusing too much on what gifts we don't have ("If only I could sing like her . . . If only I could teach a Bible study like her . . . then I'd feel good enough") leads to fear and the upside-down pride of fake humility. True humility chooses to rightly value the gifts God has given us and to use them all for his glory.

If you'd like to cultivate authentic humility in your life, let me share a handful of ways to start:

1. *Practice gratitude.* Being thankful reminds us that everything we have and everything we are comes from God. Pride and gratitude simply can't coexist. Whether you're tempted to think more highly or more lowly of yourself, gratitude aligns your perspective with the Holy Spirit.

2. *Accept compliments graciously.* This can be so difficult for us as women! True humility, however, receives recognition when it's rightly due. Saying, "Oh, it's nothing" when someone compliments the dinner you spent all day preparing isn't authentic. Talking badly about your work, always pointing out your flaws, or downplaying the gifts God has given you doesn't equal humility. Being receptive to and grateful for the encouragement others give you is an antidote to pride.

3. *Focus on serving others.* When you're busy serving others, you have less time to think about who or what you're not. If you find that you often tell yourself you have no value or that you're not capable enough or good enough, try serving. Service rights our thoughts and reminds us that we are all servants of the Lord, equal before him.

4. *Hold on loosely.* Placing your value in what you do or what you have is a recipe for pride, whether overt or disguised. You can also develop fake humility if you draw attention to yourself for being humble,

maybe by humblebragging on social media about the good works you've done for God. When we hold loosely to the things we do—and even to how God made us—we refuse to take the glory Jesus deserves.

5. *Think about what is right, true, and good.* Philippians 4:8 commands us to do this! Pride is all about *who* is right; humility focuses on *what* is right. I've observed at church that some people want you to know how much Bible knowledge they have, how well they pray, or how much they serve. Let's not walk in this kind of pride, sister! Instead of looking at who's right or who's better, let's turn our thoughts to what is right, true, and good.

6. *Memorize John 15:5.* Just before his death, Jesus told his disciples, "I am the vine; you are the branches. If you remain in me and I in you, you will bear much fruit; apart from me you can do nothing." Memorizing these words helps us remember our position before God. Humility acknowledges that we do nothing in our own strength and abilities. Only in Christ are we enough. When pride tries to sneak in, even disguised as self-congratulation for what we've done "for God," recognizing that we can do nothing apart from him keeps our hearts humble.

7. *Be willing to look at your weaknesses.* Yeah, I know that's scary. Jesus sustains us as we confront our brokenness, though. I really appreciate how blogger Lara d'Entremont describes this. She writes

that the humble woman "sees her insufficiencies, weaknesses, and lack of skill and doesn't condemn herself or become frustrated with herself. Instead, she sees it as an opportunity to learn, grow, and bring glory to God through her weakness (2 Corinthians 12:8–10). She doesn't fall into the trap of self-condemnation when she discovers sin in her life, but remembers the grace of God."[2] Isn't that so good? We don't have to be overwhelmed by weakness or self-condemnation. In Jesus we can grow and be transformed.

Which of these suggestions might you start practicing today? Don't read the words and let the opportunity pass you by. Cultivating humility is an active, deliberate choice. I'm planning to make that choice today and each day to come. Let's walk in that together, sister.

Humble Faith

As you read the Gospels, you'll find story after story of people who approached Jesus humbly and came away forever changed. God simply won't ignore a humble heart and mind. One of the stories I most cherish is found in Luke 8:42–48.

> As Jesus was on his way, the crowds almost crushed him. And a woman was there who had been subject to bleeding for twelve years, but no one could heal her. She came up behind him and touched the edge of his cloak, and immediately her bleeding stopped.

"Who touched me?" Jesus asked.

When they all denied it, Peter said, "Master, the people are crowding and pressing against you."

But Jesus said, "Someone touched me; I know that power has gone out from me."

Then the woman, seeing that she could not go unnoticed, came trembling and fell at his feet. In the presence of all the people, she told why she had touched him and how she had been instantly healed. Then he said to her, "Daughter, your faith has healed you. Go in peace."

Jesus was pressed in on every side by the large crowd following him; indeed, Luke tells us the crowd nearly crushed him. Only one person touched him in humble faith, though. Her reward? She was healed. The Greek verb *sózó*, which is translated in verse 48 as "has healed," means "to save, heal, preserve, rescue." Jesus gave this woman life, wholeness, and healing all at once. Jesus also addressed her as "daughter," a tender term that might best be translated as "dear one."

No matter what brokenness we've felt—and the woman in this story had undoubtedly endured much pain and shame throughout the twelve years of her illness—humility draws us intimately close to our Abba, our Savior. Whatever gifts we've been given by God—whether hospitality prowess like Martha, loving caregiving like Mary, or something else altogether—living with a humble heart leads to confidence in who we are. Only in exercising humility like Jesus can we ever truly know that we are enough. May we not be content to simply be near Christ, part of a crowd around him. May we actually reach out and touch him in humble faith. Life and tender love will be our reward.

Lord, you are holy, meek, and humble. You lived a life of complete surrender and obedience to your Father. I pray that you would help us, your daughters, to live a life that glorifies you through humility in choosing to serve others above ourselves. I pray for a heart position of humility for each of us. Soften our hearts to your Word and give us the courage to live according to it. As we walk through life, as we experience both trials and accomplishments, may your precious Holy Spirit guard our hearts from any pride that may rise in us. Lead us instead in your perfect way of humility. In Jesus's name, amen.

11

SET APART
THROUGH BROKENNESS

At this point in Aiden and Eliyah's young lives, the whole world is smiling at them. These boys are so loved, not just by Rashawn and me but even by perfect strangers. Their sweet smiles, their thrill in living, and their cheerful spirits are a blessing to others. They bring people joy and receive it in return.

For virtually any trouble my boys face, help is available. If they experience hunger, Rashawn and I have food to fill their little bellies. If they're tired, we have a comfortable place for them to lay their sweet little heads. If they have a boo-boo, we can kiss it better or, if things are more serious, get them help from a doctor. By the grace of God, pain can be kept to a minimum for my boys.

Of course I never want them to hurt. I'd do anything to keep them from pain. But I also know that no one gets through life without suffering. No matter how much I love them, my boys won't be an exception to this rule. It breaks my heart to think that one day they will experience pain I cannot kiss and make better, heartache that I can't fix, and suffering that I may not even be able to understand.

I pray with all my heart that through me Aiden and Eliyah will see bravery in brokenness. My desire is to set an example for them of suffering well, suffering while abiding in Jesus, serving Jesus with my giftedness even when life hurts. I hope that in their mama they will see the truth that "the Lord is near to the brokenhearted and saves the crushed in spirit" (Ps. 34:18).

Facing the continual sense of abandonment and rejection that I felt as a child and young adult changed me. I didn't even realize how much heartache had built up in me until I got married. The desire to be loved, seen, heard, and understood in ways I never had been growing up burst out of me in the early days of our marriage, often in ugly ways. I felt shocked and Rashawn felt hurt by the anger and bitterness that erupted from me when he didn't meet one of my needs or read my mind and intuitively know what I wanted.

I didn't look broken on the outside. In fact, everyone thought Rashawn and I were the perfect couple—attractive, influential, in love with Jesus and with each other. But inside I was carrying deep pain and brokenness; an internal battle raged within me.

Sister, the pain of my past, the abusive realities of my early childhood, and the way my blended family operates have often overwhelmed me, especially when I'm desperately weary—which, let's be honest, is pretty often for a mom of toddlers. Not knowing what to do with my brokenness but understanding that only God could handle it, I would retreat to my closet, fall facedown, and cry out to Jesus. In tears, I'd beg God to heal my broken heart, to restore the joy of my salvation, to rid me of the sins of bitterness and anger. When Hebrews 12:1 talks about sin that "so easily entangles us," I picture the resentment and rage that can explode out of me if I don't allow God into my pain.

Like most of you, I hate feeling broken. I'd rather live in Nehemiah 8:10 ("The joy of the LORD is your strength") than in Psalm 51:17 ("The sacrifices of God are a broken spirit; a broken and contrite heart, O God, you will not despise"; ESV). Both, however, are essential truths for our life in Christ.

Brokenness ultimately brings me closer to Jesus. It gives me a greater desire to depend on him and to love others the way he loves me. When I'm authentically aware of my messiness, I'm more gracious with others. In a way only God can bring about, goodness comes from brokenness. My gifts and abilities, when broken in the loving hands of God, actually become stronger and more glorifying to him. When I embrace brokenness, willingly feeling the pain rather than running away from it, everything I do becomes an expression of trust in the Lord, leaning on him rather than my own strength (Prov. 3:5–6). That doesn't mean pain doesn't hurt. It still does. But it also has *purpose*, and purpose transforms pain.

It probably comes as no surprise to you that we all have a choice when faced with heartache. In our brokenness, we can either run away from God or run toward him. Most of us know the so-called right answer—we should always run toward him. But how often do we actually do the opposite? I pray that in this chapter, we will see that Jesus alone is our refuge, our safety in the storms of pain and brokenness.

In order to discover that on a deeper level, let's get back to our New Testament sisters Mary and Martha and see how brokenness transformed them.

He Knows What It's Like

Mary and Martha's story doesn't end with the dinner party described in Luke 10:38–42. Though we've spent a good deal of this book looking at how that story impacts our lives as women, I want to turn now to another story that features these sisters.

We pick up their story in John 11, just a short time before Jesus's death and resurrection. Here we read that Mary and Martha's brother, Lazarus, fell gravely ill and died. Though the sisters had sent word to Jesus that Lazarus was sick and asked him to come and heal him, Jesus remained where he was a couple days longer, telling his disciples that their delay would bring greater glory to God. If you ask me, that must have been pretty confusing, not just for the disciples but also for Mary and Martha. After Lazarus died, their confusion probably dissolved into utter agony.

At the appointed time—a time only he and the Father knew—Jesus tells his disciples that it's time to travel to Bethany, where Lazarus lies entombed. Look with me at John 11:20–35, noting the powerful way this Gospel account conveys brokenheartedness.

> When Martha heard that Jesus was coming, she went out to meet him, but Mary stayed at home.
>
> "Lord," Martha said to Jesus, "if you had been here, my brother would not have died. But I know that even now God will give you whatever you ask."

Jesus said to her, "Your brother will rise again."

Martha answered, "I know he will rise again in the resurrection at the last day."

Jesus said to her, "I am the resurrection and the life. The one who believes in me will live, even though they die; and whoever lives by believing in me will never die. Do you believe this?"

"Yes, Lord," she replied, "I believe that you are the Messiah, the Son of God, who is to come into the world."

After she had said this, she went back and called her sister Mary aside. "The Teacher is here," she said, "and is asking for you." When Mary heard this, she got up quickly and went to him. Now Jesus had not yet entered the village, but was still at the place where Martha had met him. When the Jews who had been with Mary in the house, comforting her, noticed how quickly she got up and went out, they followed her, supposing she was going to the tomb to mourn there.

When Mary reached the place where Jesus was and saw him, she fell at his feet and said, "Lord, if you had been here, my brother would not have died."

When Jesus saw her weeping, and the Jews who had come along with her also weeping, he was deeply moved in spirit and troubled. "Where have you laid him?" he asked.

"Come and see, Lord," they replied.

Jesus wept.

In this story, we see the beauty of Mary's and Martha's brokenness as they grieve their dear brother. We also witness the depth of Jesus's love as he grieves with them. Jesus knew that only a few moments later he would call Lazarus from the grave and restore him to life, yet our Lord took time to weep with his beloved daughters. He comforted them with words of truth and hope. He could have simply said, "Don't cry; I'm going to make everything better." Instead, he took time to enter their brokenness. Isn't that so beautiful and hopeful?

Jesus doesn't see our heartache and say, "Get over it; I'm making all things new, so put on a happy face." He hurts with us. He understands how fragile life is for his set-apart daughters, and he willingly suffered not only *for* us but *with* us, so that we wouldn't have to remain eternally trapped in the brokenness of sin. Isaiah 53:5 makes this perfectly clear: "But he was pierced for our transgressions, he was crushed for our iniquities; the punishment that brought us peace was on him, and by his wounds we are healed." Truly, we have no hope of wholeness without the brokenness of Jesus.

This passage from John 11 reinforces the reality that, in our pain, we either can run to Jesus or run away from him. Martha and Mary initially ran to Jesus by sending him a message and requesting that he come heal their sick brother. They were familiar with Jesus's miraculous works, so they turned to Jesus as the source of hope and healing. Their Lord's delay must have been hurtful and confusing, especially given the fact that Lazarus died before Jesus arrived. Even this, however, did not stop Martha from running to Jesus as soon as he entered her hometown of Bethany.

Martha, whom we tend to judge harshly after reading Luke 10, ran to Jesus and placed herself in humility and love as close to him as possible. She affirmed his power. She acknowledged that he is the Messiah, something Jesus's twelve disciples had questioned throughout their three-year journey with him. Here in John 11, Martha shows just how much she knows, loves, and trusts Jesus, and in this story she is the one who leads Mary in sitting at his feet. I love how God reveals this about her.

It's not entirely clear from John's account whether Mary didn't know that Jesus had entered the town or whether she was simply too brokenhearted to go out and meet him along the way. We do know, however, that Martha shared the good news of Jesus's arrival with her sister, compelling Mary to follow her example and run to their Lord.

Martha and Mary recognized that Jesus could have prevented Lazarus from dying, and they both greeted him with the exact same words: "Lord, if you had been here . . ." This shows their faith in Jesus's ability and also their courage in brokenheartedness. I think it's an amazing thing that God doesn't expect us to simply accept our pain but invites us to ask him for deliverance from it instead. "I know that even now God will give you whatever you ask," Martha declared.

Our pain is not God's plan, but it is his opportunity. The Lord created this world to be perfect and painless. When sin entered the world, so did heartache. Brokenness was not God's original design, but it is a powerful vehicle of his redeeming love. In Jesus's hands, pain has purpose.

For Martha and Mary, the story of John 11 had a magnificent ending as Jesus raised their brother back to life. A miracle! What joy!

But our stories don't always end in deliverance. Sometimes they drag on in greater pain. A job loss may lead to lengthy unemployment and financial strain. A child's autism diagnosis may change the entire trajectory of a family's life. An affair may lead to a divorce, not a restored marriage. Some pain doesn't get redeemed right away. In fact, some pain persists until the end of our earthly journey.

That's why it's so essential to remember that one day all sad things will be transformed. In the end, every broken piece of our story will be placed back together. "'He will wipe every tear from [our] eyes. There will be no more death or mourning or crying or pain, for the old order of things has passed away.' He who was seated on the throne said, 'I am making everything new!'" (Rev. 21:4–5).

In the meantime, however, Jesus weeps with us. And *that* is a Savior we can trust, a Lord we can love, a heavenly Father we can run to for healing. We can also trust him to take our brokenness and make something beautiful of it. Let's look at how he does that now.

From Impossible to Unstoppable

Susi, one of my dear sisters in Christ, has faced unthinkable grief. Her beloved three-month-old baby boy died in his sleep one night. Before this tragic loss, Susi had what many would say was the perfect life, complete with a loving husband and four amazing children. When her youngest died so tragically, this sweet mama was rocked to her very core.

I cannot imagine the brokenness Susi felt. The devastation of losing a child so young and in such a seemingly senseless way touched all of us around her. Susi confessed how difficult it was for her to grasp God's love in the days after her son's death, let alone find the joy that the Bible promises is our strength.

I watched Susi mourn and grieve. She did not short-circuit that part of her journey. In Matthew 5:4, Jesus tells us, "Blessed are those who mourn, for they will be comforted." Susi's story revealed to me the truth that we must be willing to press into mourning if we long for the comfort Christ offers. We cannot stuff down or ignore the brokenness that pain brings into our lives. Instead, as we offer all the broken pieces to Jesus in mourning, we discover his presence is our comfort.

Slowly, Susi began to share about the peace God gave her moment by moment. She knew that in heaven, Jesus held her baby boy in his loving arms; her son was actually in a far better place. He had returned to the Prince of Peace, the One who had designed him, the One who loved him even more than his earthly mama could.

It didn't happen right away, but over time God began using Susi to walk alongside other women who are facing such grief. Now she regularly shares her story, strengthens others, and brings great glory to God through her pain. It may not hurt less, but Susi's pain has purpose in Jesus's plan. My sister in Christ deeply misses her little boy; no amount of time will change that. But she also displays a joy that circumstances can't take away. It's breathtakingly beautiful to behold.

Susi no longer uses the phrase "I lost my son." That has become an important distinction for her, as she firmly believes she will see her little boy again. He is not lost forever! In the meantime, she chooses to use the pain of her baby's death to glorify Jesus. Susi has gone from impossible grief to unstoppable giftedness.

Prior to that experience, Susi probably never imagined she'd be doing this kind of ministry. Truth is, none of us know how our stories will play out; most of the heartache and brokenness we experience surprises us. But some of our greatest ministry arises from the pain we endure. Without the brokenness of my past, I could not relate to God's set-apart daughters with deep empathy and love as I now do.

I don't wish pain for anyone, and I certainly wish Susi's son had not died, but intervention doesn't always make things better. We often believe that sparing others from pain will help them. That may sometimes be true; however, our good intentions may also limit a person's capacity to move from the impossible to the unstoppable.

Let's spend the last few pages of this chapter looking at how we can come alongside others as they face their own brokenness.

Calling, Command, and Privilege

Jesus spent a fair amount of time predicting hard and painful things. He also gave us incredible reasons to hope. In John 16:33, Christ declares, "I have told you these [difficult] things, so that in me you may have peace. In this world you will have trouble. But take heart! I have overcome the world." This is both good and bad news. Will there be heartache? Most definitely. Will brokenness be the end of the story? No way!

When Jesus said this, he was speaking to his twelve disciples face-to-face as friends or family members do. I believe God invites us to act in a similar way, journeying alongside others as they face the inevitable brokenness of life. It's a high calling and a great privilege to walk with the hurting, lost, and confused as God's set-apart daughters. Some of the greatest work we will ever do for God's kingdom arises from our deepest places of pain.

Here are some practical ways I believe we can allow our grief to become a place of God's giftedness:

1. *"Weep with those who weep"* (Rom. 12:15 ESV). Someone once said that two-thirds of ministry is simply showing up. Just being present with someone who's hurting can provide hope and help that gets them through another tough hour or day. Your willingness to cry with someone or even your silence might be the most precious gift you can give. There are times for words, certainly, but broken hearts often need fellowship more than instruction. Jesus cried with Mary and Martha at their brother's tomb. We can follow his example and be near to—truly *with*—others in their grief.

2. *Remind people who they are.* In this world, broken things are despised and useless, discarded and forgotten. In Jesus, brokenness is redeemed. God can take what is broken and remake it into something better, something full of his glory. Broken hearts abound for those who have been beat up by the world. Shame keeps people mired in brokenness. In love, we can remind others of their precious worth in Jesus's sight. No brokenness is too much for Jesus to mend. We can speak this truth in love to the hurting and heavy-hearted.[1]

3. *Point others back to gospel truth.* When someone is ready to talk about their hurt, it's most helpful to focus our words and their attention on Jesus. If we want to help others face their own brokenness—whether our friends, our children, or the strangers we sit next to on a plane—we do best to remind them of the gospel: God created the world in

perfection, our sin destroys and separates, God promised to rescue us, and Jesus came to fulfill that promise. His death secures eternal peace for us. "For the wages of sin is death, but the free gift of God is eternal life in Christ Jesus our Lord" (Rom. 6:23 ESV). Hurting people often need to hear that what they're going through isn't the whole story. Their story fits into a much larger battle between good and evil, hope and hell. Pointing them to the truth that we live in a broken world but have a perfect homecoming to look forward to can help. But we need to do so gently, as deeply hurting hearts can handle truth only in small doses.

4. *Love one another.* In John 13:34–35, Jesus commands us to love one another as he has loved us. What does this look like when it comes to using our giftedness to walk alongside others in their brokenness and heartache? Try starting here: remember the way Jesus entered our story, how he redeemed us from sin, and how he loves us in our brokenness. This should profoundly affect the way we treat sin in the lives of others. It should also change the way we respond to brokenness in our world. Loving others in light of Jesus's grace can be extremely challenging, but this is our call in Christ.[2] When confronted with people's sin, which leads to brokenness in their lives and perhaps in ours too, we are commanded to love as Jesus loves. By this all will know that we are his disciples.

5. *Lovingly expose false brokenness.* There are times when brokenness is used to justify sin or as an excuse for

having a victim mentality. I don't believe this honors the kind of brokenness Jesus died to redeem; rather, it keeps people in a place of heartache. I appreciate the way Anna Wishart describes this:

> It seems like brokenness can easily just become this trendy, vague word we like to slap onto our messiness and imperfection. It can become something we use to ask for pity or to describe our lives the moment we're uncomfortable. And while it's true that brokenness really is threaded intricately throughout our lives, I don't think its real meanings are found in these surface descriptions of our flawed humanity and attempts to stay "true to ourselves" by unmasking or flaunting a persona of who we think we really are.[3]

If we observe these kinds of unhealthy dynamics in someone we love, we can pray that God the Holy Spirit would open a door for us to speak into the situation. God's desire is that people be set free, not that they stay slaves to their brokenness, so we partner with the Lord when we lovingly expose false forms of brokenness. It's key in a situation like this that we are walking in step with the Spirit and following his lead as we speak into another person's life. This isn't our chance to control someone else but to be part of their hope and healing in Jesus.

Loving others in their heartache can be complex. A person may be mired in brokenness because of their own sin. Helping someone in this situation requires a great deal of discernment. A person may also be experiencing significant pain because of someone else's sin. This, too, is cause for us to seek the Holy Spirit's direction; we cannot come alongside someone in our own strength.

Sometimes a person is broken by God for their own good. These are circumstances in which we might do a great deal of damage if we step in and try to prevent the breaking. In some instances, we need to stop striving and instead passionately pray alongside someone who is being broken in the loving hands of God.

Nobody wants the people they love to experience pain, but God knows our loved ones far better than we do. He knows what is keeping them from him, what the pain in their lives might do for his glory, and how the whole story—not just your story or the stories of your loved ones, but the *entire story of all creation*—fits together perfectly.

The world is full of people with broken hearts and broken relationships. Some of those people are our parents, siblings, children, spouses, and friends. We are people in various states of brokenness.

And I'm not simply talking about physical pain. Some things inside us—pride, selfishness, anger, bitterness, idolatry—must be broken in order for us to draw closer to Jesus. Praise be to God, whether we are broken by the world or because of our own sin, God can use all brokenness for his glory.

Beloved daughter, never forget that, as Charles Spurgeon, one of the finest preachers of all time, once said, "There are many sorts of broken hearts, and Christ is good at healing them all."[4] He makes all broken things—including you and me—beautiful in his time. May we be broken enough to become beautiful for his glory.

Holy Father, *you sent your only Son to be broken for us. You, O Lord, experienced brokenness like no other. Please teach us to suffer well in this life. Holy Spirit, please comfort us in our brokenness. We long for the day when there will be a new heaven and a new earth where there will be no more pain, no more suffering, and no more crying. I pray that your joy would be our strength as we journey through this life. Please remind us that you waste no pain or suffering; we forget so easily. Thank you, God, for loving the broken areas of our lives and for continually making things new in us, and all for your glory. I praise you, Father, in Jesus's name. Amen.*

12

SET APART
FOR TODAY

PRESENT. It's a word full of possibility, isn't it?

You carefully choose and give a present to someone you love. When you're present, it can mean anything from simply being in attendance to fully engaged in where you're at or what you're doing. Put "the" in front of the word and its meaning shifts again. The present is this moment, now, right this instant.

My friend, you have been set apart by God for the present. Like Esther in the Old Testament, you have been chosen by God "for such a time as this" (Esther 4:14). And what a complicated and momentous time it is, dear one!

When I signed the contract to write this book, few people had heard of COVID-19. No one anticipated three months of stay-at-home orders or a nation divided about whether wearing masks in public spaces should be mandatory. Though many of us knew that racial tension still ran painfully deep in the United States, who could have predicted the tragedy of several brutal deaths that have led to both resistance and rioting, peaceful protests and looting? The present, this moment, now . . . there's just so much happening, isn't there?

We've been set apart in a time of great complexity. And to be honest, there have been times I've wanted to escape it all—the screaming media, the violence, the craziness and fear. While writing this book, I've been consistently tempted toward anxiety rather than trust and to worry about everything that's happening in the world—about our jobs, our family, our health, and our freedom.

When the coronavirus pandemic first unfolded in the US, I felt afraid to take Aiden and Eliyah outside the house. Rashawn and I began hosting our community group online instead of in person. As the injustice done to George Floyd, a brother created in God's image, exploded into widespread confusion and anger, I worried that our biracial family might be threatened. The present moment felt overwhelming. I didn't want all of this.

How ironic that, in the midst of writing a book about being set apart by God with unique gifting and for a glorious purpose, these toxic thoughts tried to creep into my brain. As soon as I realized the enemy was influencing my thinking, tempting me to fix my mind on the things of this earth rather than the things above, I deliberately began to take my thoughts captive and make them obedient to Christ (2 Cor. 10:5).

The Holy Spirit led me to read and meditate on Psalm 91, to abide in the secret place of the Most High and to "rest in the shadow of the Almighty." With the psalmist, I determined that "I will say of the Lord, 'He is my refuge and my fortress, my God, in whom I trust'" (Ps. 91:1–2).

Dear one, whatever is happening right now as you are reading this book, the words of this beautiful psalm bring us back to our confidence and peace in Jesus: "Surely he will save you from the fowler's snare and from the deadly pestilence. He will cover you with his feathers, and under his wings you will find refuge; his faithfulness will be your shield and rampart. You will not fear the terror of night, nor the arrow that flies by day, nor the pestilence that stalks in the darkness, nor the plague that destroys at midday" (Ps. 91:3–6). You are safe with God. You are protected. You can have peace.

Our God is faithful (Heb. 10:23). Our God is victorious (Isa. 41:10). Even though we die, yet shall we live (John 11:25). Everlasting peace and joy are our inheritance (Ps. 16:11).

Knowing and *living in* this truth changes how we view the present moment. We can trust God with the highs and lows of life. We can anchor our hope on the promises of God. Greater is he that is in us than he that is in the world (1 John 4:4). Our God will never run out of resources; he will supply all our needs according to his infinite and lavish provisions of love and grace (see Phil. 4:19).

Dear one, you have been set apart for this moment in history. Dare to use your unique gifts for the cause of Christ. Dare to courageously step out in confidence, trusting that "he who began a good work in you will carry it on to completion until the day of Christ Jesus" (Phil. 1:6).

I'd like to close our time together by giving you a glimpse of what this looks like in my daily life. I'm daring to own and use my gifting for Jesus, intentionally choosing to reject comparison and the fear of man in order to fear God and serve him more faithfully. I'm praying you'll join me in that!

Cease Striving

Thursday is my favorite day and my busiest day of the week. Rashawn and I host community group at our home every Thursday evening (barring a global health crisis, that is). I look forward to that time with our brothers and sisters in Christ all week. As I've already told you, I love welcoming people to our home. I love caring for their needs, no matter how small. When Ephesians 2:10 talks about "good works, which God prepared in advance for us to do," I know that hospitality is chief among my set-apart giftings.

If I let it, however, Thursday can also become a day of striving and stress. Whether it's striving to have the house sparkling clean, striving to get the boys bathed and fed, striving to prepare something delicious for our friends to eat, striving to clean the food stains off the floors and walls, striving to leave the best impression on people, striving to meet my husband's needs, or all of the above, I could start and finish every Thursday strive, strive, striving.

Like me, you've probably had experience with striving. Maybe it's in your workplace or even in your ministry. Maybe you strive in your parenting or with that person who's just never satisfied with what you've done or who you are. But where does all our striving lead, sister? To anxiety, frustration, and fear, right? Worried about the opinions of others. Carrying the weight of the world instead of trusting God.

I got sick and tired of how easily my favorite day could become my most destructive one. I was done with the striving. So this is what I did . . .

First, I repented of refusing to give myself grace. I acknowledged to God that I had taken everything in my own hands and left no room for him to be my strength. Repentance is always the most practical and productive thing we can do. Without true heart change, altering our behavior becomes just another form of self-reliance. I repented of my need to control every bit of my day. I confessed my complete dependence on God, not just for Thursdays but *always.*

Next, I invited God into my schedule. I actually asked the Holy Spirit—and trusted him—to guide me in specific ways. And he did! He started directing me to organize my week differently. I felt led to do things ahead of time or to release tasks altogether. Instead of deciding on my own what to do and when, I let God's voice lead me. As I did this, I was amazed how much lighter and freer I felt.

Striving stole my peace, but surrender brought it back.

My heart could remain at the feet of Jesus on Thursdays as I trusted that God knew best what I was called to do. Striving for anything outside his will would only rob me of the present moment. I could not be present for those I loved if my mind was divided by a zillion things I had strived for and failed to get done.

We read in Ephesians 2:10 God's promise that he has prepared good works for us to do—works that no one else can do! So it should come as no surprise that the enemy wants us to believe that what we're doing and how we're doing it isn't enough. Satan wants us to strive, but Jesus invites us to surrender. The enemy wants to keep us enslaved to fear, comparison, and pride, so he'll always suggest reasons why we shouldn't trust God. Remember, he used a question to tempt Eve to disbelieve her Creator: "Did God really say . . . ?" his voice hissed in her ear.

Dear one, don't allow the enemy to hiss in your ear. Silence him by choosing what is better, like our sister Mary did in Luke 10 and Martha did in John 11. Choose to stay so close to Jesus that nothing can come between you. "For I am convinced that neither death nor life, neither angels nor demons, neither the present nor the future, nor any powers, neither height nor depth, nor anything else in all creation, will be able to separate us from the love of God that is in Christ Jesus our Lord" (Rom. 8:38–39).

If nothing can separate us from Jesus's love, we can dare to step out in faith, try new things, and share our gifting with the world. We can courageously say no to fear, knowing that our God will *never* leave us or forsake us. He promises to be with us wherever we go and in whatever we do for his glory (Josh. 1:9).

God has equipped you with every tool necessary for what he's called you to do. If you have little, use it. If you have much, use it. The enemy may tempt you to worry about how big or small your giftings are, but in God's economy *all* gifts are valuable. Behind-the-scenes gifts such as prayer, encouragement, cleaning, mercy, caretaking, and anonymous generosity are not less valuable simply because they aren't seen by everyone. God designed all gifts to work together for a purpose—that his kingdom may come and his will may be done on earth as it is in heaven.

In this world, we will face times of uncertainty, not just on a global level but on the everyday level of our gifting. Jesus acknowledged this in John 16:33. Using your gifts today—or even trying to find out what they are—may feel overwhelming. I understand, sister. Let's be brave and push past this together. Let's get out of our own heads and beyond our insecurities, fixing our thoughts instead on how God can use the gifts he's given us to glorify himself and bless others.

As a precious and beloved daughter of Christ set apart for good works he prepared in advance, you can leave past failures and disappointments behind. You can let go of the fear that you don't have what it takes or that you lack the right set of skills or abilities. You may not be able to see your giftings. You may not be able to see how life can possibly be different from how it is right now. You may not see how you fit within the kingdom of God. But guess what? You don't have to see. God has called us to live by faith and not by sight (2 Cor. 5:7).

Each day offers us the choice between striving and resting, worrying and trusting, comparing and accepting. To hold one is to let go of the other.

It's time to choose a heart that is pointed toward Christ. It's time to trust him with everything that we're unsure of about ourselves and our situations. Life is about doing *all* things for God's glory, whether we're hosting people for dinner or quietly sitting at Jesus's feet. It's about daring to go to Jesus in our brokenness and then seeing that in him *we are enough just as we are.*

He has uniquely gifted each one of us, and whether you are a servant or an encourager, an evangelist or an administrator, a teacher or a prophet, a Mary or a Martha, *you are enough.* So, sister, it's time to start living like it. It's time to choose what is better—a heart postured in worship, in peace, in prayer, and in the presence of Jesus. That way, whether we're busy or silently abiding, we're always at our Savior's feet.

That's where you'll find me, sister. And that's where I pray you'll choose to be too.

Heavenly Father, *thank you for creating each one of your set-apart daughters with gifts and talents so that we might glorify you on this earth. I pray that you will reveal to each woman her gifts and give her courage to use them for your kingdom and to benefit others. I pray against the fear that may be paralyzing some women reading this book from using their gifts. Mold us and shape us into the women you've called us to be. We love you, Lord. Thank you for creating each one of us uniquely in your image. And help us to remember that you are enough for us every day. In Jesus's mighty name, amen.*

ACKNOWLEDGMENTS

SET APART would not be what it is without the support and love of the people God has sent into my life . . .

Beginning with my charming husband, Rashawn Copeland. You have truly loved me on my best days and my darkest days. Your constant support, love, and prayer have been priceless gifts to me.

To my beautiful boys, Aiden, Eliyah, and Samuel . . . you have helped me grow in ways I never thought possible. It's an honor caring for and loving you sweet boys.

To my father, David, thank you for being a voice of wisdom and instruction throughout my life. And to my mother, Lizbette, thank you for doing the best you could in raising me. I love and appreciate you both.

To the rest of my family, including Ashley, Frances, Valeria, Jan David, Alba, and all I don't have space to name . . . your love and support mean the world to me.

To my talented and skilled agent, Amanda Luedeke . . . this book could not be what it is without you. Your strength and commitment to people is beautiful and has impacted me.

To my beautiful friend, Jerusha Clark, for making this book come to life and always carrying the grace and mercy of God with you. I praise God for the wisdom he's given you.

To my outstanding editors and the rest of the family at Baker Books. Rebekah Guzman is like the older sister I never had. She is filled with life and excitement. Thank you for believing in my message for this book.

To those I would call friends, except you are more like family to me:

Al Len, for loving our family and always being a voice of grace and truth. You have been a great encouragement to me in the faith, brother.

The Maguires—Shawn, Tanda, Berk, and Hayden. You guys are the most loving and supportive family on the face of the planet. You help the Copelands grow, live, and thrive as a family. Thanks for being such great mentors and friends.

The Lewis family. Your unconditional love and encouragement have been at the center of the toughest times we've had. Your friendship is truly a treasure.

Brian C., thank you for believing and affirming me in the truth of who I am as a woman of God. You consistently challenge me to walk in my calling, and I am grateful.

The Daniels family. You guys have always cheered us on, no matter how difficult the road has been; thank you.

The Thompson family. Thank you for radiating and walking in the love of Christ.

The Earps. Thank you for demonstrating what sacrificial love looks like.

The Greys. You are a reflection of Jesus and the church. Your life and ministry are deeply valued by us.

Joanna Beck, thank you for being a strong leader and example in my walk with God. Your boldness and courage in Christ inspire me.

The Barn in Brooksville, Florida. Thank you for being obedient to God's call to reach people for Jesus.

To all whom I've crossed paths with, thank you for inviting me into your life. I love you.

And to you, Jesus, because without you I truly would not be where I am today. You are the reason for this message. I cannot take the credit, the honor, or the glory you alone deserve. Jesus, you are a friend who sticks closer than a brother. I'm praying countless hearts will be impacted as they read the message you've laid on my heart. Let this book shine a light on the beauty of being set apart for you.

NOTES

Chapter 2 Set Apart for Worship

1. Ruth Bell Graham, quoted in *The Woman's Study Bible* (Nashville: Thomas Nelson, 2012), 1281.

Chapter 4 Set Apart from Comparison

1. Henry W. Shaw, *The Complete Works of Josh Billings* (New York: G. W. Carleton & Co., 1876; Project Gutenberg, 2011), 304, https://www.gutenberg.org/files/36556/36556-h/36556-h.htm#sec-10.

2. Dictionary.com, s.v. "compare," https://www.dictionary.com/browse/compare.

Chapter 5 Set Apart from Approval-Seeking

1. Nicole Lee, "People Pleaser" (cartoon), *Doodles* (blog), July 12, 2009, https://leesdoodles.blogspot.com/2009/07/people-pleaser.html.

2. Jasmyne Lewis, personal correspondence, April 29, 2020. Used by permission.

3. The thoughts in this paragraph came from a great article by Jon Bloom, "Lay Aside the Fear of Man," Desiring God, September 16, 2016, https://www.desiringgod.org/articles/lay-aside-the-fear-of-man.

Chapter 6 Set Apart from Worry

1. John Piper, "Read the Bible to Your Anxiety," Desiring God, May 5, 2015, https://www.desiringgod.org/articles/read-the-bible-to-your-anxiety.

2. John Piper, quoted on @DesiringGod, Twitter, April 16, 2019, https://twitter.com/desiringGod/status/1118182774043828224.

3. Rashawn Copeland, Facebook post, May 3, 2019, https://www.face book.com/1191240113/posts/10216517733394446/?d=n.

Chapter 8 Set Apart in Love

1. John Piper, "How to Delight in God's Word," Desiring God, March 26, 2020, https://www.desiringgod.org/articles/how-to-delight-in-gods -word.

Chapter 9 Set Apart and Fully Known

1. For more on this, see remarks on John 2:24–25 from *Ellicott's Commentary for English Readers* and the *Pulpit Commentary* at Bible Hub, https://biblehub.com/john/2-24.htm.

2. John Piper, "Fully Known and Truly Loved," Desiring God, August 20, 2018, https://www.desiringgod.org/messages/he-knew-what-was-in -man/excerpts/fully-known-and-truly-loved; Laura Wilfer and Emily Jensen, "But This Is Just My Personality: How Christ Changes Us," *The Risen Motherhood Podcast*, episode 119, February 4, 2019, https://risen motherhood.squarespace.com/transcriptions/ep-119-but-this-is-just-my -personality-how-christ-changes-us-transcript.

3. Wilfer, "But This Is Just My Personality."

4. Piper, "Fully Known and Truly Loved."

Chapter 10 Set Apart through Humility

1. I'm indebted to Randy Conley for helping to shape my thoughts in this paragraph through his post "4 Ways to Overcome the Danger of False Humility," *Leading with Trust* (blog), October 6, 2019, https://lead ingwithtrust.com/2019/10/06/4-ways-to-overcome-the-danger-of-false -humility/.

2. Lara d'Entremont, "How to Be a Woman Clothed in Humility," *Lara d'Entremont* (blog), September 30, 2018, https://laradentremont .com/articles/a-woman-clothed-in-humility.

Chapter 11 Set Apart through Brokenness

1. You can find more on this in "What Does the Bible Say about Brokenness?," Got Questions, https://www.gotquestions.org/Bible-broken ness.html.

2. For helpful tips on talking to children about brokenness and how Jesus's love changes the way we respond to hurt and sin, see Christina Fox, "Explaining Hard Things to Our Children," The Gospel Coalition,

April 21, 2014, https://www.thegospelcoalition.org/article/explaining
-hard-things-to-our-children/.

3. Anna Wishart, "The Meaning of Brokenness in the Bible," June
11, 2019, https://e360bible.org/blog/the-meaning-of-brokenness-in-the
-bible/.

4. Charles Spurgeon, "Christ's Hospital," sermon preached at The
Metropolitan Tabernacle, March 9, 1890, https://www.ccel.org/ccel
/spurgeon/sermons38.xxiv.html.

Denisse Copeland was born and raised by a single mother in Bayamon, Puerto Rico. Her upbringing offered little stability, and Denisse soon found herself on a seemingly endless quest to find love and acceptance. It wasn't until Jesus shook her world that she truly found what she was looking for. Now a mother of two living in Oklahoma City, Denisse works alongside her husband, Rashawn Copeland, as an online minister and evangelist. Their ministry reaches more than six million people every year.

GET TO KNOW **DENISSE!**

SetApartDaughters

@ricanxo_
@setapartdaughters

@ricanxo

The Copeland's

Learn more about the Copelands' ministry, Without Walls Ministries, at **www.copelandministries.org**

LISTEN TO THE
SET APART DAUGHTERS
PODCAST

The Set Apart Daughters podcast was created to empower, encourage, and equip women to live a free and full life in Christ. So join this community of women who want to be set apart for what God has for us!

Listen on Apple Podcasts or Spotify today!